HEALTH CARE IN TRANSITION

THE "CADILLAC" TAX ON EMPLOYER HEALTH PLANS

BACKGROUND AND ANALYSES

HEALTH CARE IN TRANSITION

Additional books in this series can be found on Nova's website under the Series tab.

Additional e-books in this series can be found on Nova's website under the e-book tab.

HEALTH CARE IN TRANSITION

THE "CADILLAC" TAX ON EMPLOYER HEALTH PLANS

BACKGROUND AND ANALYSES

LESLIE CALDWELL
EDITOR

NOVINKA
New York

NOTICE TO THE READER

Library of Congress Cataloging-in-Publication Data

ISBN: 978-1-63484-246-4

Published by Nova Science Publishers, Inc. † New York

CONTENTS

PREFACE

The Patient Protection and Affordable Care Act (ACA; P.L. 111-148, as amended) included a provision to impose an excise tax on high-cost employer-sponsored insurance (ESI) coverage beginning in 2018. This provision, popularly termed the *Cadillac tax*, imposes an excise tax on ESI coverage in excess of a predetermined threshold. The tax is imposed on the coverage provider, typically the health insurance provider or the entity that administers the plan benefits. Currently, employers' spending on ESI coverage and most employees' contributions to ESI plans are exempt from income and payroll taxes. Although proposals to limit the amount of health insurance benefits eligible for this exclusion were considered, the ACA, as enacted, did not limit the exclusion for employer-provided health insurance coverage. The Cadillac tax discourages high-cost employer health plans through another approach. This book examines several issues. It evaluates the potential of the Cadillac tax to affect health insurance coverage and the health care market. It also examines the expected incidence (burden) of the tax—that is, which group's income will be reduced by the tax. Finally, the book discusses implications for economic efficiency in the context of tax administration.

In: The "Cadillac" Tax on Employer Health Plans ISBN: 978-1-63484-246-4
Editor: Leslie Caldwell

Chapter 1

The Excise Tax on High-Cost Employer-Sponsored Health Coverage: Background and Economic Analysis*

Sean Lowry

Summary

Beginning in 2018, the Patient Protection and Affordable Care Act (ACA; P.L. 111-148, as amended) imposes a 40%, nondeductible excise tax on the value of applicable employer-sponsored health coverage above specific dollar thresholds. In 2018, these thresholds are $10,200 for single health coverage and $27,500 for non-single (e.g., family) coverage. The thresholds are adjusted for eligible retirees, workers in certain high-risk professions, and plans whose demographics differ from the national workforce.

This excise tax on high-cost employer-sponsored coverage, commonly referred to as the *Cadillac tax*, is intended to raise revenue and reduce the growth of aggregate health care costs. Particularly, the Cadillac tax effectively counteracts part of the tax exclusion for

* This is an edited, reformatted and augmented version of a Congressional Research Service publication R44160, prepared for Members and Committees of Congress, dated August 20, 2015.

employer sponsored insurance (ESI), which many economists believe encourages the overconsumption of health benefits.

The Cadillac tax is estimated to raise $3 billion in 2018 and is projected to collect higher amounts of revenue each year through 2024. More plans are projected to be subject to the tax over time, because the Cadillac tax threshold is adjusted annually for inflation with the Consumer Price Index, which generally has been below the rate of growth in insurance premiums. Over the first eight years of implementation, the Congressional Budget Office (CBO) and the Joint Committee on Taxation (JCT) estimate that the tax will raise $87 billion in revenue.

As the 2018 implementation date draws closer, congressional interest in the tax has increased. For example, the Ax the Tax on Middle Class Americans' Health Plans Act (H.R. 879) and the Middle Class Health Benefits Tax Repeal Act (H.R. 2050) would specifically repeal the Cadillac tax. Opponents of the Cadillac tax argue that the tax unfairly targets certain employers' health plans because their workforce has higher health care risks. Some organized labor groups also oppose the tax because they collectively bargained for workers to receive more compensation through health benefits instead of higher wages. Proponents of the Cadillac tax argue it will help to slow the growth of national health care costs by increasing the price of excess health benefits.

Based on an analysis of employer plans in the 2013 Medical Expenditure Panel Survey Insurance Component (MEP-IC) dataset, 10.2% of single and 6.0% of non-single insurance premiums could exceed the Cadillac tax threshold in 2018 (assuming premiums grow at the same rate as their five-year averages). By 2028, 24.7% of single and 19.1% of non-single premiums could be subject to the tax. These estimates do not assume any plan modifications to avoid the tax and do not include contributions to health-related savings or reimbursement accounts. The share of plans that could be subject to the tax is sensitive to projections in premium growth rates.

INTRODUCTION

Beginning in 2018, the Patient Protection and Affordable Care Act (ACA; P.L. 111-148, as amended) imposes a nondeductible 40% excise tax on the value of *applicable employer-sponsored health coverage* above specific dollar thresholds. In 2018, these thresholds are $10,200 for single health coverage and $27,500 for non-single (e.g., family) coverage.

This excise tax on high-cost employer-sponsored coverage, commonly referred to as the *Cadillac tax*, was an important feature of the ACA for two primary reasons. One, the tax was among several revenue-raising provisions in the ACA meant to raise revenue to offset the cost of other ACA provisions (e.g., the financial subsidies available through the health insurance exchanges). Two, the tax was among several provisions intended to reduce the growth of national health care costs. Particularly, the tax is intended to target higher-cost "Cadillac" health plans (which are characterized as having more generous coverage or lower cost-sharing requirements than average health plans) and to counteract the income tax exclusion for employer-sponsored insurance's (ESI) incentives. Many economists believe ESI incentives result in the overconsumption of health benefits, resulting in upward pressure on health care costs.

Proponents of the Cadillac tax point out that employer-sponsored plans are the single largest source of health insurance coverage for the non-elderly in the United States and that the current, unlimited ESI tax exclusion (the single largest tax expenditure in the Internal Revenue Code) tends to benefit higher-income individuals more than lower-income individuals.

Critics of the Cadillac tax voice concerns that it might lead insurers to redesign their plans. Some employers claim that the tax imposes an unfair burden on their workforce because of the demographic traits of that workforce or the location of the business—not due to the generosity of their health plans. Some organized labor groups have also opposed the tax because they have negotiated collective bargaining contracts such that their members receive a larger share of their compensation in the form of health benefits in lieu of higher wages. According to these groups, the tax could disrupt these contracts such that employers' costs could increase (in the form of higher prices of the goods and services that the employers provide) or workers could bear the additional burdens of the tax (in the form of lower total compensation).

In the 114th Congress, the Ax the Tax on Middle Class Americans' Health Plans Act (H.R. 879) and the Middle Class Health Benefits Tax Repeal Act (H.R. 2050) would specifically repeal the Cadillac tax.[1]

This report gives a brief description of the Cadillac tax. It discusses the legislative origins of the tax and provides an analysis of the revenue effects of the tax. It then analyzes health insurance premium data to provide insights into what share of health insurance plans could exceed the Cadillac tax threshold and how the threshold could affect more health plans over time. This report also analyzes the Cadillac tax using standard economic criteria of efficiency, equity, and administrative simplicity.

This report is based on interpretation of the statute, and it does not consider how future regulations could affect the impact of the tax.

DESCRIPTION OF THE TAX

The ACA will impose a 40% tax on the value of *applicable employer-sponsored coverage* above a specified dollar threshold, also referred to as the *excess benefit*, beginning in 2018.[2] Applicable employer-sponsored coverage includes, but is not limited to, the following items that are subject to preferential tax exclusions:

- premiums for accident or health coverage paid by the employer or employee, and
- certain contributions to tax-advantaged accounts, such as flexible spending accounts (FSAs) and health savings accounts (HSAs).

Additionally, employer-sponsored health coverage that is paid by the employee with after-tax dollars (i.e., not subject to tax exclusion) could be included as applicable coverage.[3]

The excess benefit is calculated as the difference between the value of applicable employer-sponsored coverage and the applicable threshold level. The excess benefit is based on the aggregate cost of all employer-sponsored coverage (unless excepted). Two different thresholds apply: one for workers with single coverage, and one for workers with non-single coverage (e.g., family plans or self plus one plans).

The tax specifically does not apply to ("excepts") coverage such as long-term care insurance, stand-alone dental and vision insurance, liability insurance, and accident and disability benefits.[4] Plans provided by public employers are not excepted, and health benefits of public employees could be subject to tax.

Employers will be responsible for calculating the Cadillac tax owed for each employee's employer-sponsored coverage, as well as the share attributable to each coverage provider.[5] The tax is levied on *coverage providers*, which in some cases will be the health insurance companies that issue the employer-sponsored plans and in some cases will be the employer.[6]

The excise tax is nondeductible from the insurer's gross income (or the employer's gross income, in cases where the employer self-insures).[7] This treatment is unlike some other deductible excise taxes (such as the excise tax on medical device manufacturers) but similar to other ACA revenue-raising provisions (such as the annual fee on health insurance providers).

General Thresholds

In 2018, the threshold for calculating excess benefits will be $10,200 for single coverage and $27,500 for non-single coverage.[8] Employees in multiemployer (e.g., union) coverage will be subject only to the non-single thresholds.

In 2019, the base threshold of $10,200 (single) and $27,500 (non-single) will be indexed to the annual change in inflation, as measured by the Consumer Price Index for All Urban Consumers (CPI-U), plus one percentage point.[9] In years 2020 and beyond, the threshold will be further adjusted using only annual changes in the CPI-U. In all instances, the inflation adjustments will be rounded to the nearest multiple of $50.

Exceptions to the General Thresholds

There are several exceptions to the general thresholds. First, the thresholds are higher for retired individuals aged 55 and older who do not qualify for Medicare. For eligible plans, the threshold increases by $1,650 to $11,850 for single coverage and by $3,450 to $30,950 for non-single (or *family*) coverage.[10]

Second, there is an adjustment for certain high-risk occupations. To be eligible for the occupation exception, the plan must cover employees involved in the repair or installation of electrical or telecommunication lines, law enforcement, fire-protection activities, out-of-hospital emergency medical care (e.g., paramedics), longshore work, construction, mining, agriculture (not including food processing), forestry, and fishing industries.[11]

The same inflation adjustment used for the standard calculation of the Cadillac tax is used to adjust these modified thresholds over time.

Third, employers may also adjust the cost of the health insurance coverage if their workforce differs substantially, in terms of age and gender, from a national risk pool.[12] Regulations in this area could affect the share of plans that are subject to the tax.

LEGISLATIVE BACKGROUND

The legislative history of the Cadillac tax is rooted in efforts to limit the effects of the longstanding income tax exclusion for employer-sponsored insurance (ESI). Before discussing the specific legislative origins of the Cadillac tax, it is important to briefly review the legislative history of the ESI tax exclusion.[13]

Brief History of ESI Tax Exclusion

Since the 1920s, ESI benefits have been excluded from federal income tax. The Stabilization Act of 1942 (P.L. 77-729) further encouraged this practice through its wage controls during World War II. With wages—but not benefits—frozen, more firms began offering health benefits to attract employees. After the war, the exclusion remained in place and firms continued to offer health benefits as a fringe benefit. In 1954, the exclusion was codified in the Internal Revenue Code. ESI coverage rates have leveled off or even declined slightly since the 1960s, in part due to the creation of major programs to cover the health benefits for the poor and elderly (and subsequent expansions of such benefits).[14]

Still, ESI coverage plays a large role in the modern economy. First, employer-sponsored plans provide the largest single source of health coverage for the non-elderly population in the United States. As of 2012, 65.8% of the non-elderly population (175.4 million people) were covered by private health insurance.[15] Of that total, 88.9% (156.0 million people) were covered by an employer-sponsored plan. Second, the exclusion has become the largest single tax expenditure in the Internal Revenue Code. For FY2015, the Joint Committee on Taxation (JCT) estimates that the ESI tax exclusion is the single largest federal tax expenditure—$150.6 billion.[16]

Economic Impact of ESI Tax Exclusion in Brief

Economists note that the ESI tax exclusion can both increase and decrease economic efficiency as well as decrease the perceived "fairness" or equity of the income tax. Incentives for ESI could enhance economic efficiency because ESI provides a risk-pooling mechanism that is unrelated to health factors among the working population. Further, ESI could reduce health costs through increased bargaining power and decreased administrative costs.[17] In contrast, studies have concluded that the tax exclusion for ESI encourages greater health care consumption than would be the case without a tax preference, thus generating an economically inefficient outcome.[18]

In addition to the debate over economic efficiency, the ESI tax exclusion changes the burden distribution of the income tax. Generally, the ESI exclusion is regressive, since the exclusion is more valuable to those in higher income brackets.[19] Individuals who obtain coverage outside of an employer-sponsored plan or uninsured workers generally do not benefit from the ESI tax exclusion.

Congressional Discussions on Reforming the ESI Tax Exclusion

Economists and policy experts discussed the merits and potential options for eliminating the ESI tax exclusion over the course of a three-session Senate Finance Committee roundtable discussion held in spring 2009 (one year before enactment of the ACA).[20] In one opening statement, Senate Finance Chairman Max Baucus said

> We should also look at the current tax treatment of health care. I know that there is some controversy about doing so. Some do not want to modify the current unlimited exclusion for employer-provided health care, and I agree that we are not going to eliminate that exclusion. But the current tax exclusion is not perfect. It is regressive and often leads people to buy more health coverage than they need...We should look at ways to modify the current tax exclusion so that it provides the right incentives, and we should look to ways to make it fairer and more equitable for everyone.[21]

Members of the Senate Finance Committee and a bipartisan panel of health care experts discussed several issues within the context of limiting or eliminating the ESI tax exclusion in 2009, including

- limiting the exclusion for certain taxpayers above a particular income;
- limiting the exclusion for the value of plans over a percentile of the average actuarial value of employer-sponsored plans;[22]
- adjusting any limit for regional difference in plans or for age of the workforce;[23]
- what types of health benefits should be tax preferred (e.g., HSAs, FSAs);[24] and
- how to adjust the limit over time.[25]

Legislative Origins of the Cadillac Tax

The idea of the Cadillac tax emerged in legislation as part of the chairman's mark of the America's Healthy Future Act of 2009, the Senate Finance Committee's draft bill for health care reform, released on September 16, 2009.[26] This first version of the Cadillac tax would have taxed insurance policies with excess benefits above a threshold ($8,000 for single plans and $21,000 for family plans) at a rate of 35% beginning in 2013.[27] The Congressional Budget Office (CBO) and the JCT estimated that the provision would have raised $215 billion over the budget window from 2010 to 2019 (i.e., within the first seven fiscal years of implementation). The threshold would have been adjusted for inflation in 2014 and beyond. This version of the bill also included a three-year transition rule that would have increased the threshold for the 17 highest-cost states.

On September 22, 2009, the modified chairman's mark was released, and the Senate Finance Committee began to mark up the bill over seven days.[28] The modified mark increased the Cadillac tax rate to 40%, but it adjusted the threshold in 2014 and beyond for changes in inflation plus one percentage point. The initial threshold amounts were not modified. The Cadillac tax provision in the modified mark was estimated by CBO and JCT to raise $201 billion over the budget window (i.e., $14 billion less than the initial version).

On December 19, 2009, CBO and JCT released analysis of S.Amdt. 2786, a substitute for the House-passed Affordable Care Act (H.R. 3590). The version of the Cadillac tax in this bill had higher thresholds ($8,500 singles, and $23,000 family policies) than the Senate version, but retained the higher 40% tax rate and the adjustment for inflation plus one percentage point.[29] This version of the Cadillac tax would remain intact until the ACA was approved by Congress on March 21, 2010.

On March 20, 2010, CBO and JCT released analysis of the Health Care and Education Reconciliation Act (HCERA), an amendment to the provisions in the ACA. In particular, HCERA delayed the implementation of the Cadillac tax from 2013 to 2018 and raised the thresholds ($10,200 for singles, and $27,500 for families). CBO and JCT scored the revised Cadillac tax as raising $32 billion from 2010 to 2019 (i.e., after the first two years of implementation). The House passed the Senate-modified ACA and HCERA on March 21, 2010, and the Senate passed the bill (which eventually became P.L. 111-148) by reconciliation on March 25, 2010.

After enactment, bipartisan concerns emerged. These concerns culminated in a letter organized by Representative Joe Courtney and Representative Tom

Cole opposing the Cadillac tax and any provision intended to reduce the benefits associated with the ESI tax exclusion.[30]

Estimated Revenue Effects of the Cadillac Tax

In April 2014, CBO and JCT estimated that the Cadillac tax will raise $5 billion in FY2018 and will collect higher amounts of revenue each year through FY2024.[31] Over the first *seven* years of implementation, CBO and JCT estimated that the tax will raise $120 billion in revenue.[32]

In March 2015, CBO and JCT significantly reduced their most recent estimates of the Cadillac tax to indicate that the tax will raise $87 billion over the first *eight* years of implementation (FY2018 to FY2025).[33] Because premium growth is now projected to be slower, fewer workers are expected to enroll in employment-based insurance plans whose costs exceed the excise tax thresholds specified in the ACA.[34]

In comparison, CBO and JCT estimated in March 2015 that two other provisions in ACA, the employer penalty and the individual mandate, will raise $145 billion and $34 billion, respectively, over the same eight-year period (FY2018 to FY2025). The $3 billion projected to be raised by the Cadillac tax in FY2018 is also small relative to the estimated $172 billion annual tax expenditure associated with the tax exclusion for ESI in that same year.[35]

Official scores indicate that the Cadillac tax will raise revenue directly on applicable plans exceeding the threshold and indirectly through increases in taxable income for employers that reduce health benefits and increase wages. Roughly one-quarter of the revenue gain stems from excise tax receipts, and roughly three-quarters stems from a net increase in employees' taxable compensation and, to a lesser extent, in employers' deductible expenses.[36] This assessment assumes that employers will shift compensation over time from health benefits to wages to reduce or avoid the Cadillac tax.

Share of Plans with Insurance Premiums Exceeding the Tax's Threshold

This section of the report analyzes insurance premiums to provide insights into what share of insurance premiums exceed the Cadillac tax threshold.

These premiums are a major component of health plan coverage as defined by ACA, but they are not the only component of coverage. Thus, the Cadillac tax could affect more health plans over time than estimated here if all components of applicable coverage are included. Note that the estimates also assume no further changes are made by employer providers to avoid or reduce exposure to the tax. Other studies are reviewed in the *Appendix* of this report.

In June 2015, the Congressional Research Service (CRS) requested that the Department of Health and Human Services' (HHS's) Agency for Healthcare Research and Quality (AHRQ) estimate the share of premiums that could have a health insurance premium greater than the applicable Cadillac tax threshold. At the request of CRS, AHRQ used the 2013 Medical Expenditure Panel Survey Insurance Component (MEP-IC) dataset, which is a sample of plans provided by 39,216 private-sector establishments and public employers.[37] CRS provided AHRQ with Cadillac tax thresholds adjusted for CBO's projected annual changes in the CPI-U between 2018 and 2038.[38] CRS then asked AHRQ to simulate the growth of insurance premium values offered by employers in the MEPS-IC data. These scenarios are based on different historical trends exhibited by the cost of the average insurance premium found the Kaiser Family Foundation's (KFF's) and the Health Research & Educational Trust's 2014 Employer Health Benefits Survey.[39] The scenarios include

- "Lower Growth": assuming an annual growth rate in average insurance premiums of 4.6% for single coverage and 4.7% for family coverage, based on a five-year average of trends within the KFF data.
- "Moderate Growth": assuming an annual growth rate in average insurance premiums of 5.0% for single coverage and 5.4% for family coverage, based on a 10-year average of trends within the KFF data.
- "Higher Growth": assuming an annual growth rate in average insurance premiums of 7.0% for single coverage and 7.4% for family coverage, based on a 15-year average of trends within the KFF data.

The analysis at the state level is provided using only the lower-growth scenario, given the low probability that insurance premium growth by 2018 will increase to rates seen more than a decade ago. In contrast, analyses of the Cadillac tax at the national level are plotted according to all three growth scenarios. While it is uncertain that insurance premium growth will reach the rates in the moderate- to high-growth scenarios, these scenarios illustrate how changes in the actual rate of insurance premium growth can affect the number of premiums subject to the tax.

A full description of the data and methodology used to derive these illustrations appears in the *Appendix*.

Caution should be exercised when interpreting some state results due to potential estimation issues stemming from smaller sample sizes and significant variation in premium amounts in some states.[40]

The estimates of the share of premiums that exceed the Cadillac tax threshold provided in this section of the report should not be conflated with analysis of how many plans could actually be subject to the Cadillac tax. This analysis only includes insurance premiums and does not include the costs of other types of coverage that count toward the threshold (e.g., certain contributions to FSAs and HSAs).[41]

Additionally, any estimate of the share of premiums affected by the Cadillac tax is subject to a number of uncertainties.

- First, the growth rate of premium costs has generally been declining in recent years.42 The analysis in this report models different assumptions in the potential growth of health care costs. Additionally, the analysis in this section of the report does not imply that each scenario is equally likely; rather, this analysis illustrates how sensitive estimates of the Cadillac tax are to inflation projections. Estimates of the impact of the tax using older data could overestimate the actual increase in average health insurance costs in more recent years. Future insurance premium growth rates could continue slowing, or could deviate from the trends used here.
- Second, it is uncertain how employers will respond (or have already responded) to the tax.43 Since the tax was enacted in 2010, some employers have already begun to offer less generous plans (thus, some behavioral effects would already be contained within observed data).44 For example, employers could offer a high-deductible health plan, which might be less likely to cross the threshold than their traditional PPO/HMO plan. The analysis in this section assumes that employers do not take any actions to adjust the plans offered to employees.
- Third, this report does not take into consideration how regulations could affect implementation of the tax. Treasury and IRS could issue regulations clarifying the benefits potentially subject to tax, safe harbors for employers, and modifications in various cost adjustments

(e.g., under the workforce age and gender provision). Regulations in these areas could reduce (or increase) the number of plans subject to the tax.

2018

Figure 1 and *Figure 2* depict the share of single and non-single plans, respectively, with premiums that could exceed the tax in 2018, by state.

As shown in *Figure 1*, approximately 10.2% of single premiums, nationally, could be subject to the tax in 2018. As shown in *Figure 2*, approximately 6.0% of non-single premiums, nationally, could be subject to the tax in 2018.

It should be noted that the following figures do not provide insight into what share of a plan's health benefits is subject to tax or the amount by which the plan exceeds the threshold. Only the portion of health benefits in excess of the threshold is subject to tax. Additionally, these figures do not quantify how many enrollees in these plans could be affected.

(under the assumption of 4.7% annual premium growth, in individual plans)

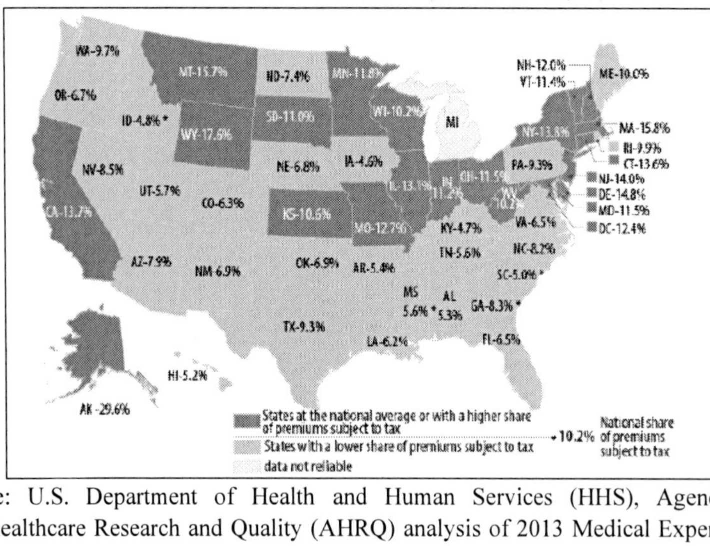

Source: U.S. Department of Health and Human Services (HHS), Agency for Healthcare Research and Quality (AHRQ) analysis of 2013 Medical Expenditure Panel Survey-Insurance Component (MEPS-IC) data provided to the Congressional Research Service (CRS) in June 2015.

Notes: All reported values have a standard error (SE) of less than 2% and a relative standard error (RSE) of less than 30%. Caution should be taken when interpreting the results with an asterisk (*), which denotes an RSE of greater than 25%. Any estimate with an RSE greater than 30% is considered unreliable and omitted from this graphic. Reported values are weighted by the number of plans in the data sample. This graphic does not take into account any exceptions to the general Cadillac tax threshold for certain "high-risk" professions or for employers with workforces that differ from the age and gender profile of the national risk pool. See report text for more details.

Figure 1. Percentage of Employer-Sponsored, Single Premiums Estimated to Exceed the Cadillac Tax Threshold in 2018, by State. (under the assumption of 4.7% annual premium growth, in individual plans)

(under the assumption of 4.6% annual premium growth, in family plans)

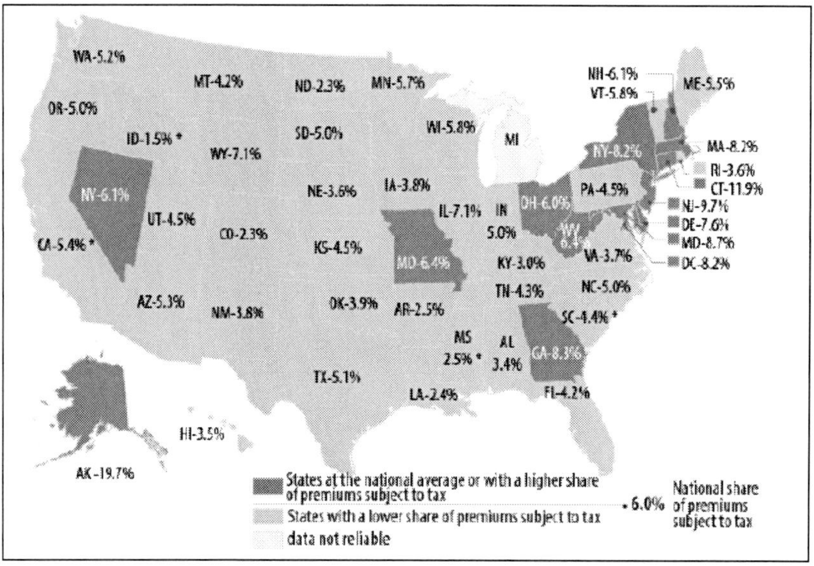

Source: AHRQ analysis of 2013 MEPS-IC data provided to CRS in June 2015.

Notes: All reported values have a standard error (SE) of less than 2% and a relative standard error (RSE) of less than 30%. Caution should be taken when interpreting the results with an asterisk (*), which denotes an RSE of greater than 25%. Any estimate with an RSE greater than 30% if considered unreliable and omitted from this graphic. Reported values are weighted by the number of plans in the data sample. This graphic does not take into account any exceptions to the general Cadillac tax threshold for certain "high-risk" professions or for employers with workforces that differ from the age and gender profile of the national risk pool. See report text for more details.

Figure 2. Percentage of Employer-Sponsored, Non-Single Premiums Estimated to Exceed the Cadillac Tax Threshold in 2018, by State.

2019 and Beyond

Figure 3 and *Figure 4* show the national share of single and non-single premiums, respectively, that could be subject to the Cadillac tax over time. The share of premiums that could be subject to the Cadillac tax is estimated to increase over time, primarily because the growth of inflation in the CPI-U (which is used to adjust the Cadillac tax threshold) is projected to increase more slowly than the historical trends for premium growth.

Figure 3 shows that between 2018 and 2028, the share of single premiums that could be subject to the Cadillac tax increases from 10.2% to 24.7% under the lower-growth scenario. *Figure 4* shows that between 2018 and 2028, the share of non-single premiums that could be subject to the Cadillac tax increases from 6.0% to 19.1% under the lower-growth scenario. For both single and non-single premiums, the share of plans affected by 2028 is higher under the moderate- and higher-growth scenarios.

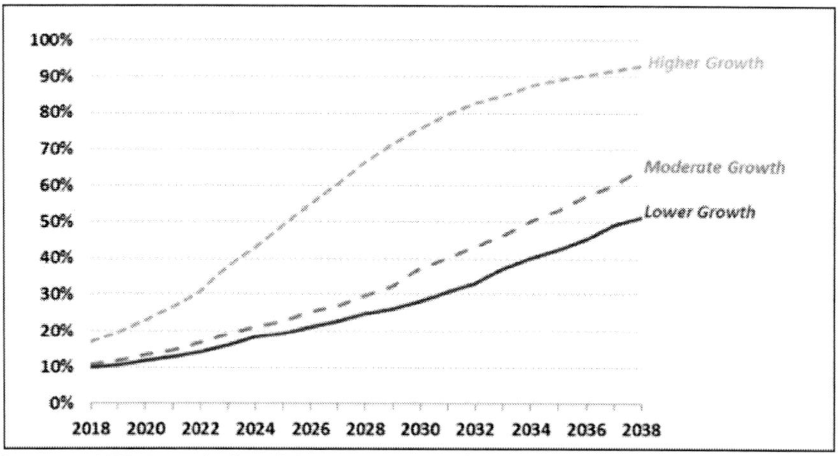

Sources: AHRQ analysis of 2013 MEPS-IC data provided to CRS in June 2015; growth rates in the different scenarios are derived from historical average premium values from Kaiser Family Foundation (KFF), 2014 Annual Survey of Employer Health Benefits, September 10, 2014, at http://kff.org/health-costs/report/2014-employerhealth-benefits-survey/; and projections of the Consumer Price Index for All Urban Consumers (CPI-U) from the Congressional Budget Office, The Budget and Economic Outlook: 2015 to 2025, January 26, 2015, at https://www.cbo.gov/publication/45066.

Notes: "Lower Growth" scenario assumes annual growth in average health insurance premiums of 4.6%, based on a 5-year average in historical trends; "Moderate Growth" scenario assumes an annual growth rate of 5.0%, based on a 10-year average; and "Higher Growth" estimate assumes an annual growth rate of 7.0%, based on a 15-year average. Historical trends are averaged from KFF data. Regarding the tax threshold, trends in the CPI-U are held constant at 2024 levels for years outside of CBO's projection window (i.e., 2025 to 2038). See Appendix for more details on methodology. This graphic does not take into account any exceptions to the general Cadillac tax threshold for certain "high-risk" professions or for employers with workforces that differ from the age and gender profile of the national risk pool. See report text for more details.

Figure 3. Percentage of Employer-Sponsored, Single Premiums Estimated to Exceed the Cadillac Tax Threshold, Nationally, 2018-2038.

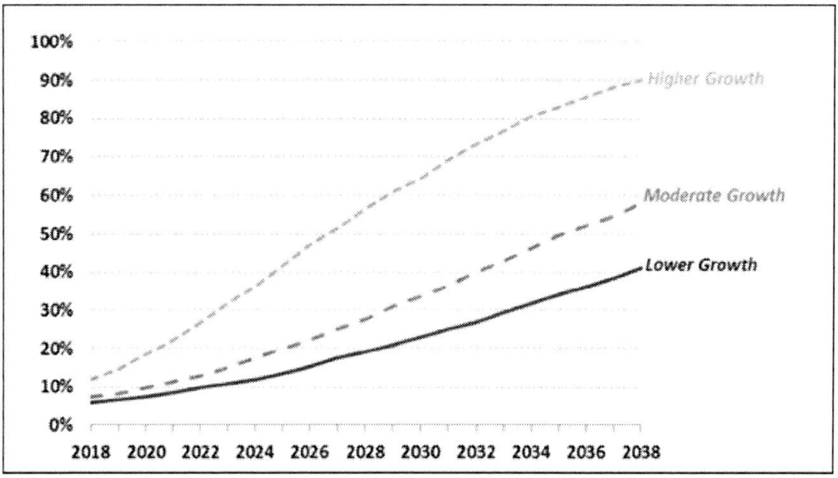

Sources: AHRQ analysis of 2013 MEPS-IC data provided to CRS in June 2015; growth rates in the different scenarios are derived from historical average premium values from KFF, 2014 Annual Survey of Employer Health Benefits, September 10, 2014, at http://kff.org/health-costs/report/2014-employer-health-benefits-survey/; and projections of the CPI-U from the CBO, The Budget and Economic Outlook: 2015 to 2025, January 26, 2015, at https://www.cbo.gov/publication/45066.

Notes: "Lower Growth" scenario assumes annual growth in average health insurance premiums of 4.7%, based on a 5-year average in historical trends; "Moderate Growth" scenario assumes an annual growth rate of 5.4%, based on a 10-year average; and "Higher Growth" estimate assumes an annual growth rate of 7.4%, based on a 15-year average. Historical trends are averaged from KFF data. Regarding the tax threshold, trends in the CPI-U are held constant at 2024 levels for years outside of CBO's projection window (i.e., 2025 to 2038). See Appendix for more details on methodology.

This graphic does not take into account any exceptions to the general Cadillac tax threshold for certain "high-risk" professions or for employers with workforces that differ from the age and gender profile of the national risk pool. See report text for more details.

Figure 4. Percentage of Employer-Sponsored, Non-Single Premiums Estimated to Exceed the Cadillac Tax Threshold, Nationally, 2018-2038.

Interaction of the Cadillac Tax and a Hypothetical Employer-Sponsored Plan

In contrast to the aggregate analysis in *Figure 3* and *Figure 4,* the graphs in this section of the report illustrate how a hypothetical employer-provided plan could be subject to the tax over time. *Figure 5* and *Figure 6* chart a hypothetical, preferred provider organization (PPO) plan for single and non-single coverage, respectively. The plan provides a comprehensive scope of benefits (physician's visits, pharmaceutical, vision, dental, etc.). The major characteristics of this plan are that it has no deductible, charges flat fees for doctor's visits and prescriptions, and does not cover medical care outside of the preferred provider network. For more information on the methodology used to construct this illustration, see the *Appendix.*

The 2015 premiums are adjusted over time using the same three growth scenarios used in previous figures.

As shown in *Figure 5*, this hypothetical employer-provided single plan would be subject to the Cadillac tax in 2033 under the lower-growth scenario. In the moderate- and higher-growth scenarios, the hypothetical plan would be subject to the tax in an earlier year. As shown in *Figure 6*, the non-single plan would be subject to the Cadillac tax in 2038 under the lower-growth scenario (or earlier under the moderate- or higher-growth scenarios).

Interaction of the Cadillac Tax and Small Group and Small Business (SHOP) Insurance Exchange Plans

In addition to the general effect of applying to more employer-sponsored plans, the tax, left unadjusted, could also affect small group plans. Small group plans include the employer-sponsored plans that are part of the Small Business Health Options Program (SHOP) exchanges.[45] SHOP exchanges are marketplaces where small employers can purchase health insurance plans from health insurance issuers.

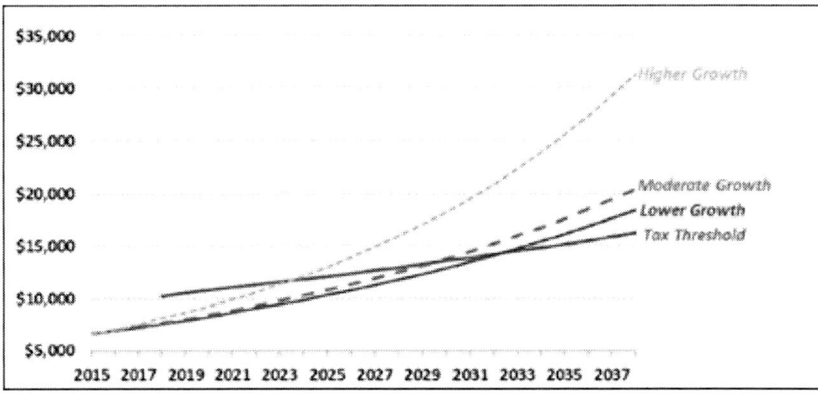

Sources: CRS analysis of historical average premium values from KFF, 2014 Annual Survey of Employer Health Benefits, September 10, 2014, at http://kff.org/health-costs/report/2014-employer-health-benefits-survey/; and projections of the CPI-U from the Congressional Budget Office (CBO), The Budget and Economic Outlook: 2015 to 2025, January 26, 2015, at https://www.cbo.gov publication/ 45066.

Notes: "Lower Growth" scenario assumes annual growth in average health insurance premiums of 4.6%, based on a 5-year average in historical trends; "Moderate Growth" scenario assumes an annual growth rate of 5.0%, based on a 10-year average; and "Higher Growth" estimate assumes an annual growth rate of 7.0%, based on a 15-year average. Historical trends are averaged from KFF data. Regarding the tax threshold, trends in the CPI-U are held constant at 2024 levels for years outside of CBO's projection window (i.e., 2025 to 2038). See Appendix for more details on methodology.

Figure 5. Illustration of the Long-Term Interaction of the Cadillac Tax Threshold and the Premium for a Hypothetical Employer-Provided Single Plan.

This effect could reduce the incentive for businesses to offer plans in the SHOP exchanges, if it is less expensive for their employees to obtain similar coverage in the individual exchanges (or the workers could forgo health insurance and potentially face the individual mandate penalty).[46] If an employer with at least 50 full-time-equivalent (FTE) employees does not offer at least a *bronze plan*, defined as having an actuarial value of 60%, and at least one worker receives a tax credit or subsidy in the individual exchanges, then the employer could be subject to the ACA's employer penalty.[47]

National data on average premiums in the SHOP exchanges is limited, and only plan-specific premium data is available from official sources.[48] With this said, it is unlikely that these less generous plans in the SHOP exchanges will be subject to the Cadillac tax in the foreseeable future, given that the silver- and bronze-level plans in the SHOP are less generous than the hypothetical plan analyzed in the "Interaction of the Cadillac Tax and a Hypothetical Employer-Sponsored Plan" section this report.

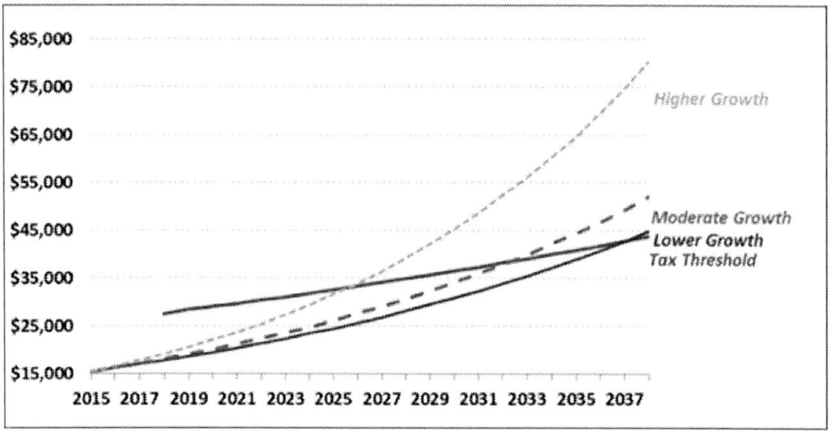

Sources: CRS analysis of historical average premium values from KFF, 2014 Annual Survey of Employer Health Benefits, September 10, 2014, at http://kff.org/health-costs/report/2014-employer-health-benefits-survey/; and projections of the CPI-U from the CBO, The Budget and Economic Outlook: 2015 to 2025, January 26, 2015, at https://www.cbo.gov/publication/45066.

Notes: "Lower Growth" scenario assumes annual growth in average health insurance premiums of 4.6%, based on a 5-year average in historical trends; "Moderate Growth" scenario assumes an annual growth rate of 5.0%, based on a 10-year average; and "Higher Growth" estimate assumes an annual growth rate of 7.0%, based on a 15-year average. Historical trends are averaged from KFF data. Regarding the tax threshold, trends in the CPI-U are held constant at 2025 levels for years outside of CBO's projection window (i.e., 2026 to 2038). See Appendix for more details on methodology.

Figure 6. Illustration of the Long-Term Interaction of the Cadillac Tax Threshold and the Premium for a Hypothetical Employer-Provided Non-Single Plan.

ECONOMIC ANALYSIS

This section analyzes the Cadillac tax using standard criteria for evaluating tax policy: economic efficiency, equity, and administrative simplicity. However, because the Cadillac tax is often compared to limits on the tax exclusion for ESI under current law, the two policies are also compared.

Economic Efficiency

The health care sector contains many sources of market failures, some of which create economic inefficiencies.[49] The inefficiency that is most directly related to the Cadillac tax is the moral hazard issue of those with health insurance. In general, insured individuals spend more on medical care than they would without insurance. More demand for medical care raises the price of medical care, and insurance and cost-sharing subsidies could insulate individuals from the full cost of their health-related decisions.[50] Incentives that encourage insurance consumption, such as the ESI tax exclusion, can increase these inefficiencies in the market for medical care.[51] The Cadillac tax is intended in part to reduce this source of inefficiency.

Economic Incidence of the Tax

For the purposes of the Cadillac tax, there are two important levels of analyzing who bears the economic burden of the tax. First, there is a determination of how the added costs of the Cadillac tax are passed along from the plan administrator to covered employees. Second, there is a determination of which share of this cost is borne by employees versus medical care providers (e.g., hospitals, doctors, drug companies).

It can be expected that much of the economic burden of the Cadillac tax will be passed along to labor, much like any other partial tax on a factor of production.[52] This analysis is for employers that offer "Cadillac" health plans as part of their total employee compensation package. Since the tax increases the relative cost of one form of labor compensation (health benefits), it follows that the tax will shift the mix of compensation offered by some employers more toward wages (which become relatively less expensive after the tax is enacted).

Higher wages are likely preferable for most workers, since health benefits above the tax threshold are subject to a marginal tax rate of 40% plus any insurer markups to offset higher income tax payments due to the higher, post-Cadillac tax price of health benefits. In contrast, most workers will be facing a marginal tax rate on wages less than the top income tax rate of 39.6% plus the 7.65% employee portion of the payroll tax.[53] Some workers, who are more risk-averse and value the after-tax value of an additional one dollar of health benefits versus wages, may still want to retain their health plans even if part of the plan is subject to the Cadillac tax.[54]

This analysis, above, reflects the *long-term* effects on labor markets. In the short run, wages are sometimes "sticky" and bound by the terms of particular contracts or labor agreements. Indeed, some industries that have rigid labor contracts might be slower to adjust than others. With this said, some employers negotiating multi-year, collective bargaining agreements might already be trying to price the effects of the tax into labor contracts prior to 2018.

Effects on the Market for Medical Care

The Cadillac tax's effects on the mix of compensation taken up by employees also have effects on the market for medical care, depending on the sensitivity of producers and consumers to changes in price.

A standard supply and demand market framework can used to better understand how the Cadillac tax could affect the market for medical care. The demand for most goods and services is inversely related to the price of that good, such that consumers demand less of a good or service when prices are higher. In contrast, the supply of most goods and services is positively related to price, such that suppliers produce more of a good or service when prices are higher.

In a world without insurance, consumers face the full price of medical care and demand an amount of medical care. When insurance is introduced, individual consumers pay a share of their full medical care costs and then demand a higher amount of medical care at this insurance-subsidized price. Other subsidies for health insurance, such as the ESI tax exclusion, further contribute to reductions in the price faced by consumers. After introducing insurance (and any other subsidies), the quantity of medical care demanded is higher than it would have been absent insurance or other cost-sharing or cost-reduction incentives.

The Cadillac tax is designed to increase the price of medical care above the tax's threshold, such that the price of this care to consumers is closer to the full (or true) cost of their medical care. On net, the demand for medical care after imposing the tax is still above the quantity demanded under the full market price (since insurance and subsidies still exist), but less than the quantity demanded after incorporating the effects of insurance and subsidies without the tax. In practice, the tax increases the cost-sharing burden on consumers for medical care over the threshold for those employees and employers who choose to reduce insurance coverage. For plans that are modified in order to avoid the tax, these cost-sharing increases could come in a variety of forms of higher out-of-pocket costs (e.g., higher co-payments, deductibles, or other features).

It is this decrease in medical care spending that will purportedly lead to reduced costs in the overall medical care market, relative to a world without the tax. As medical care above the threshold level becomes more costly, spending on medical care will decrease and spending on other commodities will increase.

The exact magnitude of this market change is unknown. First, the underlying data on the growth of health care spending are changing. If the growth of insurance costs continues to increase at a pace less than recent historical trends, then it is likely that the Cadillac tax will affect fewer plans than projected (and result in fewer savings on medical care expenditures). Additionally, the size of the change in the market depends on how responsive consumers and producers are to changes in price.[55] As discussed in *The Excise Tax on High-Cost Employer-Sponsored Health Insurance: Estimated Economic and Market Effects*, by Jane G. Gravelle, the Cadillac tax, under certain assumptions, could lead to an overall decline in national health expenditures of 0.6%-0.9% in 2018 and by 2.5%-3.6% in 2024. In other words, the tax could result in a gross reduction of $7.6-$11.0 billion in national health expenditures in 2018 and $41.0- $60.3 billion by 2024.

Repealing or capping the tax exclusion for ESI could have effects on economic efficiency similar to those of the Cadillac tax. However, there could be efficiency tradeoffs to consider when looking at options for implementing such a cap. A major administrative issue impeding the taxation of employer-sponsored health care benefits is measuring the imputed value of health benefits received. Some measures of a health plan's value are now available on an employee's W2 form, but this amount could be closer to an average cost per worker across an employer's workforce and does not necessarily represent the *ex post* health benefits received by the particular taxpayer.[56] If workers were subject to taxation on the full cost of their health benefits received, then higher-risk workers would face a higher tax penalty under an ESI tax exclusion cap. These workers are more likely to be elderly or other groups more likely to use health care. If workers were subject to an approximate measure of health benefits, such as the average benefit received across an employer's workforce, then relatively healthy workers would subsidize less healthy workers. Although the latter case might be desirable under a social insurance principle, it could raise issues about equity across different types of taxpayers.

Equity

Mermin and Toder (2015), researchers at the Tax Policy Center, find that if the Cadillac tax were repealed and premiums reverted back to their pre-Cadillac tax levels, taxpayers with incomes between $50,000 and $200,000 would experience a 0.3 percentage point decrease in their average tax rate by 2025 compared to current law (that assumes the Cadillac tax comes into effect in 2018).[57] Taxpayers below and above this income range would experience a smaller change in their average tax rate. These distributional effects are similar to previous analyses of the tax.

JCT analyses of preliminary versions of the Cadillac tax indicate that the tax's effects are primarily concentrated among middle- and upper-middle-income taxpayers. JCT modeled the distributional effects of earlier versions of the Cadillac tax found in the America's Healthy Future Act of 2009 (S. 1796), as reported by the Senate Finance Committee in October 2009, and the version of the Affordable Care Act (H.R. 3590) passed by the House in December 2009.[58] In summary, analysis of the more recent, House-passed version showed that the tax resulted in an increase, at most, of 0.1 percentage points in the average tax rate (defined as federal taxes paid divided by adjusted gross income) within a particular income range in the first year of implementation, and up to a 0.3 percentage points in the average tax rate within a particular income range in the seventh year of implementation.[59] In the House-passed version, the largest change in average tax rates (0.3 percentage points) was estimated to occur among taxpayers with incomes between $50,000 and $200,000.

Distributional analysis of the ESI tax exclusion indicates that it is regressive (and repealing the ESI tax exclusion would increase progressivity).[60] The tax benefits of the exclusion tend to increase with income until the highest income levels (where income grows faster than health benefits). According to Treasury analysis, the ESI tax exclusion results in tax benefits, at most, of 2.4% of after-tax income in 2015.[61] The largest changes in relative income due to the ESI tax exclusion accrue to those with $47,339 and $113,139 in income (i.e., the 60th to 90th percentiles of the income distribution). It is difficult to make a nuanced comparison of the two policies at the upper end of the income distribution, since the income ranges used by JCT and Treasury are different. Overall, though, the ESI tax exclusion's distribution of the tax benefits as a share of after-tax income is roughly similar to the distribution of the Cadillac tax's increases in average tax rates.

The Cadillac tax may be viewed by some as violating the principle of horizontal equity, which states that the tax code should treat like-situated taxpayers similarly. Health premiums are often more expensive for reasons beyond an individual's control. Thus, taxpayers with similar income levels and expected health care consumption could be subject to disproportionate federal tax burdens, simply because their health plans have characteristics that are more likely to trigger the Cadillac tax. For example, higher premiums in certain geographic areas could be due to higher claims rates, riskier industries, differences in health professional practice styles, large distances between care providers, older populations, etc. Furthermore, there might be wide variation in premiums within a particular state.

The Cadillac tax provides a mechanism to adjust, at least in part, for some of the demographic variation in health premiums. First, professionals in certain industries and qualified retirees above 55 years old are subject to a higher threshold. Second, the dollar limits for an employer's plan are increased if the age and gender characteristics of the employer would result in higher premiums than those of the national workforce (as measured by the Federal Employee Health Benefits Program's Blue Cross and Blue Shield standard benefit option). It remains to be seen whether the inflation, age and gender, and other adjustments provided in statute will keep workers with these special circumstances from paying the tax (at least in the short run).

Alternative policies that limit the tax exclusion for ESI might also pose complications for those who wish to promote tax equity. It is difficult to calculate the imputed value of an individual's health benefits, as mentioned in the "Economic Efficiency" section of this report. If workers were taxed the average value of their health benefits (which is how they are currently calculated on workers' W-2s by some firms), then younger and risk averse individuals would effectively be subsidizing older and less risk averse individuals. If the true value of an individual's health benefits were reported on a W-2, it is likely that older workers or workers with higher health risk profiles would receive more health benefits (and be subject to higher income taxes) than younger workers or workers with relatively lower health risk profiles.

Administrative Simplicity

In general, the tax has created a degree of administrative complexity as employers continue to develop and implement strategies to avoid or minimize their Cadillac tax burden. Meanwhile, the Treasury and IRS are still issuing regulatory guidance on the tax, as of the publication date of this report.[62]

Policies to limit or to cap the tax exclusion for employer-sponsored insurance (ESI) could modify the existing reporting requirement to specify the full range of employer-sponsored health benefits that lawmakers wish to make taxable.[63] Although this option would more accurately report the value of an individual's health benefits, it could create additional compliance costs for employers, employees, and insurance administrators. Additionally, those who would pay the most in taxes under this form of administration could be more likely to need health coverage; increasing the cost of these health benefits could create disincentives for them to utilize insured medical care.

CONCLUSION

Although it is among one of the last ACA provisions to come into effect, the Cadillac tax is on track to become one of the most salient features of the ACA. The tax is estimated to raise $3 billion in 2018, but annual tax collections are expected to increase to $87 billion by 2026.

Absent significant changes in the trajectory of insurance premium costs or types of health plans offered by employers, the Cadillac tax is expected to apply to a greater share of employer-sponsored health plans over time. Changes in the trajectory of premium costs primarily affect when, not if, the Cadillac tax will apply to most health plans, as they are structured today. If premium costs increase at a slower rate than in recent history, then the share of plans affected by the tax would likely fall below current estimates (and vice versa).

As employers modify the types of health plans that they offer their employees, they are likely to offer more compensation in the form of wages, which are subject to income and payroll taxes, and less in the form of health benefits. This reduction in health benefits could materialize in a number of different ways, many of which would increase the cost-sharing burden of medical care costs on employees.

By increasing out-of-pocket costs for "excess benefits" above the tax's threshold, the tax intends to reduce demand for medical care above a certain insurance premium value. It is this reduction in demand that could reduce the growth rate in national health care spending, relative to a world without the tax.

APPENDIX. ANALYTICAL REVIEW AND METHODOLOGY

Selected Studies and Surveys Estimating the Effects of the Cadillac Tax

Prior studies have estimated a range of possible effects of the tax, including the share of private insurance plans that could be subject to the tax, strategies that employers are considering or adopting to avoid the tax, and the revenue raised by the tax.

Herring and Lentz (2012) estimated the number and characteristics of plans that would likely be affected by the tax in 2018 and beyond.[64] The authors projected the excise tax threshold forward, and use data from the 2008-2009 Kaiser Family Foundation (KFF) Employer Health Benefits Survey to estimate the percentage of plans exceeding the excise tax threshold in each year.[65] Employees from both public and private employers are included in the KFF dataset. Multiple estimates are provided, based on various assumptions to insurance premium growth rates (ranging from 4.5% to 7.5% per year). According to Herring and Lentz's analysis, 6.6% of single plans and 6.3% of family-of-four plans are estimated to exceed the threshold in 2018, and 29.4% of single plans and 30.2% of family-of-four plans are estimated to exceed the threshold in 2029 (under an assumption of a premium growth rate of 4.5% per year).[66] Summary statistics for plans exceeding the threshold in 2018 are provided along different plan characteristics (e.g., preferred provider organization versus health maintenance organization, employee characteristics, employer and industry characteristics, and geographic area of the plan).

According to a presentation by Mercer, a business consultancy, on March 16, 2015, 31% of employers surveyed said they would be subject to the tax in 2018 if they made no changes to their current plans.[67] Likewise, 51% of firms surveyed said they would be affected by 2022.[68] Among survey respondents, 48% said they implemented a "consumer-driven health plan" (CDHP), 38% said they were steered more employees into a CDHP, 28% said they raised deductibles of other cost-sharing provisions, and 17% said they dropped high-cost plans. Among survey respondents 48% were considering raising deductibles or other cost-sharing provisions, 34% were considering dropping high-cost plans, 23% were considering implementing a CDHPs, and 22% were considering steering more employees into CDHPs.[69]

In November 2014, the American Health Policy Institute (AHPI) released a study of the potential impacts of the Cadillac tax.[70] Based on a January and February 2014 survey of over 350 large companies that are members of the Human Resources Policy Associations, AHPI reported that more than 38% of respondents would be affected by the tax in 2018 unless they made changes to their plans.

Methodology and Detailed Results Estimating the Share of Plans Subject to the Cadillac Tax

To project the Cadillac tax's thresholds over time, the 2018 statutory thresholds of $10,200 (single) and $27,500 (family) in 2018 are inflated for years 2019 to 2024 using the Congressional Budget Office's (CBO) projections of annual changes to the Consumer Price Index for all Urban Consumers (CPI-U).[71] For years 2025 to 2038, the annual growth in the CPI-U in the last year of CBO's projection is held constant.[72] Increases in the actual rate of inflation in the CPI-U reduce the share of premiums subject to the Cadillac tax over time.

Table A-1. Assumed Annual Growth Rates in Illustrated Cases of Growth in Average Annual Health Insurance Premiums

Scenario	Historical Trend	Single Coverage	Family Coverage
"Lower Growth"	Last 5 years	4.6%	4.7%
"Moderate Growth"	Last 10 years	5.0%	5.4%
"Higher Growth"	Last 15 years	7.0%	7.4%

Source: CRS analysis of Kaiser Family Foundation (KFF) data.

Notes: "Lower Growth" scenario is averaged over the five-year period from 2010 to 2014, "Moderate Growth" scenario is averaged over the ten-year period from 2005-2014, and "Higher Growth" scenario is averaged over the 15-year period from 2000 to 2014.

Health insurance premiums in the 2013 Medical Expenditure Survey Insurance Component (MEPS-IS) dataset are inflated on an annual basis using three different scenarios based on historical trends in average health insurance premiums are derived from the KFF Annual Employer Survey.[73] As shown in

Table A-1, the "Lower Growth" scenario averages the annual growth rates over the past 5 years for single and family coverage, respectively; the "Moderate Growth" scenario averages annual growth rates over the past 10 years; and "Higher Growth" scenario averages annual growth rates over the past 15 years.

Methodology for Estimating a Hypothetical Employer-Provided Premium and the Cadillac Tax Threshold

Figure 5 and Figure 6 illustrate the intersection between a hypothetical employer-provided insurance premium and the Cadillac tax threshold. This report bases this illustration on the 2015 premiums from the "basic" option Blue Cross and Blue Shield (BCBS) plan found in the Federal Employee Health Benefits Plan (FEHBP).[74] This plan was chosen for the purposes of this analysis because it is subscribed to by many workers and ample data concerning enrollments and plan characteristics are available.[75]

It is important to note that the figures in this section of the report should be interpreted as illustrations only, and are *not* intended to be a projection of the effects of the Cadillac tax on the FEHBP's BCBS plans over time.[76] The plans represented in the subsequent analysis are also not necessarily representative of the majority of private-sector, employer-sponsored plans.

End Notes

[1] H.R. 879, the Ax the Tax on Middle Class Americans' Health Plans Act, would also repeal certain health coverage cost reporting requirements in Internal Revenue Code (IRC) §6051(a).

[2] In other words, the tax only applies to the amount of coverage exceeding the threshold.

[3] See IRC 4980I(d)(1)(A) through (D): The term "'applicable employer-sponsored coverage' means ... coverage under any group health plan made available to the employee by an employer which is excludable from the employee's gross income under section 106, or would be so excludable if it were employer provided coverage ... without regard to whether the employer or employee pays for the coverage." Additionally, Treasury and the Internal Revenue Service (IRS) have further clarified this interpretation in a request for information. See IRS, Notice 2015-16, February 23, 2015, at http://www.irs.gov/pub/irs-drop/n-15-16.pdf: "Section 4980I(d)(1)(C) provides that coverage that meets the basic definition of applicable coverage is applicable coverage 'without regard to whether the employer or employee pays for the coverage.' In addition, coverage that otherwise meets the definition of applicable coverage is applicable coverage without regard to whether the employer

provides the coverage (and thus the coverage is excludable from the employee's gross income) or the employee pays for the coverage with after-tax dollars."

[4] For a full list of exceptions, see IRC §4980I(d)(1)(B). For more detailed list of health benefits that could be subject to the Cadillac tax and information on areas in which Treasury intends to issue regulations, see IRS, Notice 2015-16, February 23, 2015, at http://www.irs.gov/pub/irs-drop/n-15-16.pdf.

[5] See p. 4 in ibid.; IRS, Notice 2015-52, July 30, 2015, p. 7, at http://www.irs.gov/pub/irs-drop/n-15-52.pdf; "Excise Tax on 'Cadillac' Plans," Health Affairs, September 12, 2013, at http://www.healthaffairs.org/healthpolicybriefs/ brief.php?brief_id=99; National Insurance Services, Inc., "Cadillac Tax on High-Cost Health Coverage," Health Care Reform legislative brief, at http://www.nisbenefits.com/ppaca/18- Legislative%20Brief% 20 Cadillac%20Tax%20on%20High%20cost%20Health%20Coverage%20102213.pdf; and Cigna, Cadillac Tax Fact Sheet, January 2015, at http://www.cigna.com/assets/docs/about-cigna/informed-on-reform/ cadillac-tax-fact-sheet.pdf.

[6] IRC Section 4980I(c).

[7] Although the cost of the tax, itself, is nondeductible, IRS has issued regulations defining which costs "attributable the tax" are excluded from the calculation of the "applicable coverage" tax base. This would include higher costs charged by third-party insurers to account for higher income tax payments resulting from receipts on plans subject to the tax. See IRS, Notice 2015-52, July 30, 2015, p. 7, at http://www.irs.gov/pub/irs-drop/n-15-52.pdf.

[8] Employee-plus-one plans, which typically provide coverage for an employee and a spouse, would be subject to the non-single coverage threshold. In other words, the Cadillac tax threshold for non-single plans does not distinguish between these employee-plus-one plans and family coverage. Additionally, statute requires that the 2018 thresholds are adjusted by the health cost adjustment percentage, which is a one-time upward adjustment if premium growth in the Blue Cross Blue Shield (BCBS) Standard Plan offered through the Federal Employees Health Benefit (FEHB) program exceeds a certain percentage. It is unlikely that the 2018 thresholds will be subject to the adjustment, so this report does not consider the impact of the potential adjustment when discussing the 2018 thresholds.

[9] IRC §4980I(b)(3)(C)(v).

[10] IRC §4980I(b)(3)(C)(iv).

[11] IRC §4980I(f)(3). See the IRC for specific definitions of each profession.

[12] The FEHB BCBS Standard plan is used to make age and gender adjustments. See IRC Section 4980I(b)(3)(C)(ii). For further clarification regarding multiple employers under common control (e.g., multiple franchises owned by the same individual), see IRC Section 4980I(f)(9). Statute requires that the 2018 thresholds be adjusted by the health cost adjustment percentage. The health cost adjustment percentage is a one-time upward adjustment based on premium growth in the FEHB BCBS Standard plan. The 2018 dollar limits will be adjusted upward if premium growth in the BCBS Standard plan is more than 55% between 2010 and 2018. It is unlikely that the 2018 thresholds will be subject to the adjustment, so this report does not consider the impact of the potential adjustment when discussing the 2018 thresholds. For more discussion, see IRS, Notice 2015-52, July 30, 2015, p. 7, at http://www.irs.gov/pub/irs-drop/n-15- 52.pdf.

[13] For a more in-depth discussion, see CRS Report R40834, The Market Structure of the Health Insurance Industry, by D. Andrew Austin and Thomas L. Hungerford.

[14] For more background, see Employment and Health Benefits: A Connection at Risk, ed. Marilyn J. Field and Harold T. Shapiro (Washington, DC: National Academy Press, 1993), p. 27.

[15] Employee Benefit Research Institute (EBRI), Sources of Health Insurance and Characteristics of the Uninsured: Analysis of the March 2013 Current Population Survey, EBRI Issue Brief #390, September 2013, at http://www.ebri.org/publications/ib/index.cfm? fa=ib Disp& content_id=5272. Although EBRI has yet to update this analysis for 2013 data, the U.S. Census Bureau has published 2013 coverage data for "working-age adults" (aged 19 to 64) in Jessica C. Smith and Carla Medalia, Health Insurance in the United States: 2013 (Current Population Reports), U.S. Census Bureau, September 2014, at https://www.census.gov/ content/dam/Census/library/publications/2014/demo/ p60-250.pdf.

[16] Joint Committee on Taxation (JCT), Estimates of Federal Tax Expenditures for Fiscal Years 2014-2018, JCX-97-14, August 5, 2014, p. 31, at https://www.jct.gov/ publications. html?func=startdown&id=4663. Note that the tax expenditure is only calculated based on losses to income tax revenue. It does not include revenue lost from payroll taxes for Social Security and Medicare if this form of compensation was taxed like wages.

[17] For more explanation about the rationale of the employer-sponsored insurance (ESI) system, see CRS Report R43181, The Affordable Care Act and Small Business: Economic Issues, by Sean Lowry and Jane G. Gravelle. The benefits to ESI have become less pronounced after enactment of the Patient Protection and Affordable Care Act (ACA; P.L. 111-148, as amended), in part due to the new insurance exchanges, market reforms, premium tax credits, and cost-sharing subsidies.

[18] See Jonathan Gruber and James M. Poterba, "Tax Subsidies to Employer-Provided Health Insurance," in Empirical Foundations of Household Taxation, ed. Martin Feldstein and James Poterba (Chicago, MA: University of Chicago Press, 1996), pp. 135-169.

[19] The degree of regressiveness is reduced, however, when the exclusion from payroll taxes, which are partially capped for higher-income earners, is considered. Further, when measured as a share of after-tax income, the ESI exclusion is fairly flat for lower- and middle-income earners, and decreases for higher-income earners. Since health insurance premiums do not tend to rise much with income, the distribution of ESI exclusion benefits is flatter than the distribution of income. See Congressional Budget Office (CBO), The Distribution of Major Tax Expenditures in the Individual Income Tax System, Washington, DC, May 2013, at https://www.cbo.gov/sites/default/files/113th-congress-2013-2014/ reports/43768_DistributionTaxExpenditures.pdf.

[20] U.S. Congress, Senate Committee on Finance, Roundtable Discussion on Expanding Health Care Coverage, 111th Cong., 1st sess., May 5, 2009, pp. 114-167, at http://www. finance.senate.gov/hearings/hearing/?id=d8c677d4-fa54- 11f2-1c31-64fbd9076f32.

[21] Ibid., p. 115.

[22] Ibid., p. 125. See comments by Senator Max Baucus: "we can dial this any way we want. Basically my understanding is that the average in business is about the 75th or 76th percentile of actuarial value that companies now provide for their employees."

[23] Ibid., p. 142. This was an issue of reoccurring economic and legal interest during the roundtable session. Most notably, Dr. Len Burman, Director of the Urban Institute's Tax Policy Center, suggested that "if you could design an efficient health insurance plan and figure out what costs would be in each state and tie a cap to that, that would be the ideal cap. A second-best measure might be to take something like the lowest-cost plans in the Federal Employees Health Benefit Program, which vary across States, and you could tie the cap to that."

[24] For the discussion on flexible savings accounts (FSAs), see ibid., pp. 133-134. For the discussion on health savings accounts (HSAs), see ibid., pp. 150-151.

[25] Ibid., p. 166. See comments by the Gail Wilensky, Senior Fellow at Project HOPE: "As long as it is not indexed to medical expenditures it will begin to have more impact over time."

[26] For the CBO analysis of the preliminary version of the bill, see Letter from Douglas Elmendorf, Director of the Congressional Budget Office, to Hon. Max Baucus, Chairman of the Senate Committee on Finance, September 16, 2009, at http://www.cbo. gov/publication/41265?index=10572.

[27] The chairman's mark also factored tax-excluded spending arrangement and health savings accounts into the calculation of excess benefits like the final provision.

[28] See Senate Committee on Finance, Modifications to the Chairman's Mark "America's Healthy Futures Act of 2009, September 22, 2009, at http://finance.senate. gov/download/ ?id=900c6417-5bb5-4cc6-a67d-911cac22e35b. On October 7, 2009, CBO and JCT released analysis of the modified chairman's mark of the America's Healthy Future Act. See Letter from Douglas Elmendorf, Director of the Congressional Budget Office, to Honorable Max Baucus, Chairman of the Senate Committee on Finance, October 7, 2009, at http://www.cbo.gov/publication/41335.

[29] See Letter from Douglas Elmendorf, Director of the Congressional Budget Office, to Hon. Harry Reid, Majority Leader of the US Senate, December 19, 2009, at http://www. cbo.gov/sites/default/files/12-19- reid_letter_managers_correction_noted.pdf.

[30] See Letter from Reps. Joe Courtney and Tom Cole to Members of the Senate Finance Committee and House Ways and Means Committee, November 4, 2011.

[31] CBO, Insurance Coverage Provisions of the Affordable Care Act—CBO's March 2015 Baseline, March 9, 2015, at https://www.cbo.gov/sites/default/files/cbofiles/ attachments/ 43900-2015-03-ACAtables.pdf.

[32] CBO, Updated Estimates of the Effects of the Insurance Coverage Provisions of the Affordable Care Act, April 2014, p. 2, at https://www.cbo.gov/sites/default/files/45231-ACA_Esti mates.pdf.

[33] CBO, Updated Budget Projections: 2015 to 2025, March 2015, at https://www. cbo.gov/sites/default/files/cbofiles/attachments/49973-UpdatedBudget Projections.pdf.

[34] Ibid., p. 9 and 19.

[35] JCT, Estimates of Federal Tax Expenditures for Fiscal Years 2014-2018, JCX-97-14, August 5, 2014, p. 31, at https://www.jct.gov/publications.html?func=startdown&id=4663.

[36] CBO, Updated Estimates of the Effects of the Insurance Coverage Provisions of the Affordable Care Act, April 2014, p. 13, at https://www.cbo.gov/sites/default/files/45231-ACA_ Estimates.pdf.

[37] Agency for Healthcare Research and Quality, "MEPS-IC Sample Size," at http:// meps.ahrq. gov/mepsweb/ survey_comp/ic_sample_size.jsp.

[38] Annual changes in the Consumer Price Index for All Urban Consumers (CPI-U) were taken from CBO's Long-Term Budget and Economic Outlook. For more information, see the Appendix.

[39] The Kaiser Family Foundation (KFF) surveys both private and public employers, but the data limit KFF's ability to analyze public employees. For more information on the sample design of the KFF survey, see Kaiser Family Foundation, "Methodology–2014 Employer Health Benefits Survey," at http://kff.org/report-section/ehbs-2014- methodology/.

[40] The reliability of the sample mean relative to the actual population mean (the standard error of the mean) and the variability or precision of the measurement (the relative standard error) are different for each state. For example, a standard error of the mean (SEM) of 1% indicates that the standard deviation is 1% above or below the sample mean. Estimates with lower relative standard errors (RSE) can be said to have a more precise measurement,

because they have proportionately less sampling variation around the mean. Estimates where the RSE is greater than 30% are omitted from this report's analysis because they are considered statistically unreliable, as per the standards set forth in Richard J. Klein et al., "Health People 2010 Criteria for Data Suppression," Center for Disease Control (CDC), National Center for Health Statistics, Healthy People 2010, July 2002, at http://www.cdc.gov/nchs/data/statnt/statnt24.pdf.

[41] Some studies have tried to incorporate these benefits into estimates of the impact of the Cadillac tax (See the description of Herring and Lentz, 2012, in the Appendix). It is uncertain how data on these benefits in a world before the Cadillac tax might be representative of a world after the tax is implemented. Contributions to these accounts are easier to adjust than changes in annual premiums. These other accounts could lead to excess benefits above the Cadillac tax threshold (thereby making more plans subject to the tax) or they could allow some employees on the margins of the threshold to reduce their contributions to a level that their total excess benefits would not rise above the threshold.

[42] See Table A-1.

[43] For anecdotal evidence of one employer, Harvard University, already making changes to its employee health plans, see Robert Pear, "Harvard Ideas on Health Care Hit Home, Hard," New York Times, January 5, 2015, at http://www.nytimes.com/2015/01/06/us/health-care-fixes-backed-by-harvards-experts-now-roil-its-faculty.html.

[44] The JCT's analysis of the tax assumes that, over time, employers will offer less generous health plans in exchange for higher wages.

[45] The Cadillac tax only applies to employer-sponsored plans. Thus, plans purchased by individuals in the marketplace would not be subject to the Cadillac tax. For more information on the SHOP exchanges, see CRS Report R43771, Small Business Health Options Program (SHOP) Exchange, by Annie L. Mach.

[46] For more background, see CRS Report R41331, Individual Mandate Under the ACA, by Annie L. Mach, and CRS Report R43181, The Affordable Care Act and Small Business: Economic Issues, by Sean Lowry and Jane G. Gravelle. Individuals without ESI could face additional economic incentives to not purchase health care, because health coverage purchased by individuals (in individual markets, like the exchanges) is not subject to the same, tax-excluded status as ESI. Under current tax law, taxpayers may only deduct contributions to their health premiums if they itemize tax deductions and their total medical and dental costs are greater than 10% of their adjusted gross income.

[47] For more information, see CRS Report R43981, Affordable Care Act (ACA): Employer Shared Responsibility Determinations and Potential Penalties, by Julie M. Whittaker.

[48] In contrast, official summaries of average premiums on the individual health exchanges are available in publications, such as Office of the Assistant Secretary for Planning and Evaluation (ASPE), Department of Health and Human Services (HHS), Health Plan Choice and Premiums in the 2015 Health Insurance Marketplace, January 8, 2015, pp. 16-17, at http://aspe.hhs.gov/health/reports/2015/premiumreport/healthpremium2015.pdf. ASPE only analyzes premiums from 35 states that are not state-based exchanges. For a more in-depth discussion of ASPE's methodology, including its weighting techniques, see the notes to Table 10 in Health Plan Choice and Premiums in the 2015 Health Insurance Marketplace.

[49] Some of these inefficiencies are summarized in Joseph Stiglitz, Economics of the Public Sector, 3rd ed. (New York: Norton), pp. 300-330; and Executive Office of the President, Council of Economic Advisers, The Economic Case for Health Care Reform, June 2009, pp. 9-17, at https://www.whitehouse.gov/assets/documents/ CEA_Health_Care_Report.pdf.

[50] Joseph Stiglitz, Economics of the Public Sector, 3rd ed. (New York: Norton), p. 315.

[51] ESI can also reduce other inefficiencies in the health care market. For more discussion, see CRS Report R43181, The Affordable Care Act and Small Business: Economic Issues, by Sean Lowry and Jane G. Gravelle.

[52] For a similar comparison, see the incidence analysis of the federal payroll tax in Harvey S. Rosen, Public Finance, 7th ed. (New York, NY: McGraw-Hill Irwin, 2005), pp. 285-287.

[53] This is a very simplified calculation of comparing marginal tax rates, and does not take into consideration other factors, such as: the cap on wages subject to the Social Security part of the federal payroll tax, any state and local income tax rates, or any federal deductions for state and local taxes paid. For more detailed analysis on the incidence of the tax, see CRS Report R44159, The Excise Tax on High-Cost Employer-Sponsored Health Insurance: Estimated Economic and Market Effects, by Jane G. Gravelle.

[54] According to the Joint Committee on Taxation (JCT), most employers and workers will shift to plans that are not subject to the Cadillac tax. See Letter from Thomas A. Barthold, Chief of Staff, Joint Committee on Taxation, to the Hon. Joe Courtney, U.S. House of Representatives, October 16, 2009, p.2. This assumption was reaffirmed in CBO, Updated Estimates of the Effects of the Insurance Coverage Provisions of the Affordable Care Act, April 2014, p. 13, at https://www.cbo.gov/publication/45231.

[55] An elasticity of demand for insured health services of -0.2 is commonly referred to in the health economics literature. In other words, a 10% increase in the price of medical care leads to a 2% decline in the quantity of health care demanded by consumers. For example, see Su Liu and Deborah Chollet, Price and Income Elasticity of the Demand for Health Insurance and Health Care Services: A Critical Review of the Literature, Mathematica Policy Research, Inc., March 24, 2006, at http://www.mathematica-mpr.com/publications/pdfs/priceincome.pdf. Although some economists caution the use of a single elasticity to describe all medical spending, studies of different types of medical care often find demand to still be relatively inelastic (i.e., less than 1.0 in absolute value terms). The supply responses are expected to be relatively elastic (greater than 1.0). For further discussion of the supply elasticities, see CRS Report R44159, The Excise Tax on High-Cost Employer-Sponsored Health Insurance: Estimated Economic and Market Effects, by Jane G. Gravelle.

[56] For a discussion of the problems associated with imputing income from employer health benefits see Stan Dorn, Capping the Tax Exclusion of Employer-Sponsored Health Insurance: Is Equity Feasible?, June 2009, at http://www.urban.org/sites/default/files/alfresco/publication-pdfs/411894-Capping-the-Tax-Exclusion-of-EmployerSponsored-Health-Insurance-Is-Equity-Feasible-.PDF.

[57] See Gordon Mermin and Eric Toder, Distributional Impact of Repealing the Excise Tax on High-Cost Health Plans, Tax Policy Center, July 2015, at http://www.taxpolicycenter.org/UploadedPDF/2000315-Distributional-Impact-ofRepealing-the-Excise-Tax-on-High-Cost-Health-Plans.pdf. For a separate attachment, see Table T15-0103, at http://taxpolicycenter.org/numbers/Content/PDF/T15-0103.pdf.

[58] For analysis of the Senate Finance Committee's America's Healthy Future Act of 2009, see Letter from Thomas A. Barthold, Chief of Staff, Joint Committee on Taxation, to the Hon. Joe Courtney, U.S. House of Representatives, October 16, 2009. For analysis of the version of the ACA passed by the House in December 2009, see Letter from Thomas A. Barthold, Chief of Staff, Joint Committee on Taxation, to the Hon. Joe Courtney, U.S. House of Representatives, December 8, 2009.

[59] See Letter from Thomas A. Barthold, Chief of Staff, Joint Committee on Taxation, to the Honorable Joe Courtney, U.S. House of Representatives, October 16, 2009. These exact

estimates, however, are likely to be outdated due to newer data regarding inflation, discontinuation of some of the affected insurance policies, changes in current law income tax policy, and other behavioral changes in anticipation of the tax. In addition, the current law tax policy baseline changed since 2009 with the enactment of permanent, marginal income tax rates in the American Taxpayer Relief Act of 2012 (P.L. 112-240).

[60] For example, taxpayers in the top 20% of the income distribution account for 34% of the tax expenditure value for the ESI tax exclusion. See Congressional Budget Office, The Distribution of Major Tax Expenditures in the Individual Income Tax System, May 2013, pp. 14-15, at https://www.cbo.gov/sites/default/files/43768_DistributionTax Expenditures.pdf. Generally, a tax exclusion provides a higher tax benefit for those facing higher marginal tax rates (in contrast to a tax credit, which is a dollar-for-dollar offset against tax liability regardless of income). The share of the tax expenditure value for the ESI tax exclusion tends to decline among the highest income earners, though, as income grows faster than health insurance. At the bottom of the income distribution, lower-income workers are more likely to work part-time and are typically not offered employer-sponsored health coverage. Additionally, the Tax Policy Center finds similar distributional effects of limiting the ESI tax exclusion.

[61] U.S. Department of the Treasury, Office of Tax Analysis, Distribution of Selected Income Tax Expenditures: Tax Benefits as a Share of After-Tax Income, July 28, 2014, at http://www.treasury.gov/resource-center/tax-policy/Documents/Analysis-and-Research-Selected-Credits-Deductions-Exclusions-2015.pdf.

[62] For more information, see IRS, Notice 2015-16, February 23, 2015, at http://www.irs.gov/pub/irs-drop/n-15-16.pdf; and IRS, Notice 2015-52, July 30, 2015, at http://www.irs.gov/pub/irs-drop/n-15-52.pdf

[63] For a list of employer-sponsored health benefits are currently subject to reporting, see Internal Revenue Service, "Form W-2 Reporting of Employer-Sponsored Health Coverage," at http://www.irs.gov/Affordable-Care-Act/Form-W2-Reporting-of-Employer-Sponsored-Health-Coverage. Currently, employers can pick one of multiple ways to calculate the amount of health benefits listed on an individual's W-2, but not all of them measure the actual value of health benefits received by the individual. For more information, see Internal Revenue Service, Notice 2012-9, at http://www.irs.gov/pub/irs-drop/n-12-09.pdf.

[64] Bradley Herring and Lisa Korin Lentz, "What Can We Expect from the 'Cadillac Tax' in 2018 and Beyond," Inquiry, vol. 48 (Winter 2011), pp. 322-337.

[65] The authors also used data from other sources to model employer contributions to HSAs, HRAs, and FRAs as part of their base of applicable coverage.

[66] Ibid., p.326.

[67] "Impact of the Excise Tax on Employer Sponsored Coverage," a presentation by Tracy Watts before a lunch panel in the Rayburn House Office Building, March 16, 2015. Data from this presentation was derived from Mercer's 2015 report, Health Care Reform Five Years In, and Mercer's National Survey of Employer-Sponsored Health Plans 2014.

[68] Just because an employer is "affected" by the tax, though, does not mean that all of their offered plans are affected.

[69] Consumer-driven health plans (CDHPs) include high-deductible health plans with an HSA or health reimbursement account (HRA).

[70] See Tevi D. Troy and D. Mark Wilson, The Impact of the Health Care Excise Tax on U.S. Employees and Employers, American Health Policy Institute, November 10, 2014, at http://www.americanhealthpolicy.org/Content/documents/resources/Excise_Tax_11102014.pdf.

[71] See CBO, The Budget and Economic Outlook: 2015 to 2025, February 2015, p. 6, at https://www.cbo.gov/sites/ default/files/45010-Outlook2014_Feb_0.pdf. To derive the 2019 threshold projection, one percentage point is added to CBO's projected annual increase in the CPI-U.

[72] From 2020 to 2025, CBO projects that the CPI-U will grow at an annual rate of 2.3%. For the purposes of the projections in this report, growth in the CPI-U is held constant at an annual rate of 2.3% in years 2026 to 2038. Actual inflation rates could vary.

[73] This data is typically shown as Exhibit 1.11 in the KFF annual publications. For the most recent edition of the report, see Kaiser Family Foundation (KFF), 2014 Annual Survey of Employer Health Benefits, September 10, 2014, at http://kff.org/health-costs/report/2014-employer-health-benefits-survey/.

[74] For more information of the plan characteristics, see Blue Cross and Blue Shield, "Plan Brochures," at https://www.fepblue.org/en/benefit-plans/benefit-plans-brochures-and-forms/.

[75] The BCBS options had the highest take-up rates among active, non-Postal Service government employees participating in the FEHB in 2014, based on CRS analysis of data provided by the Office of Personnel Management (OPM) on June 4, 2015. In 2014, approximately 32.2% of non-Postal Service, federal employees enrolled in a FEHB single plan and 35.4% of non-Postal Service, federal employees enrolled in a FEHB non-single plan were enrolled in the BCBS basic option. Approximately 32.7% of non-Postal Service, federal employees enrolled in a FEHB single plan and 33.0% of non-Postal Service, federal employees enrolled in a FEHB non-single plan were enrolled in the BCBS standard option.

[76] For example, the annual premium growth in these FEHBP BCBS plans has been lower than the average growth rates exhibited in the KFF data. Additionally, the demographics of the federal workplace could be different than most employers.

In: The "Cadillac" Tax on Employer Health Plans ISBN: 978-1-63484-246-4
Editor: Leslie Caldwell

Chapter 2

THE EXCISE TAX ON HIGH-COST EMPLOYER-SPONSORED HEALTH INSURANCE: ESTIMATED ECONOMIC AND MARKET EFFECTS*

Jane G. Gravelle

SUMMARY

The Patient Protection and Affordable Care Act (ACA; P.L. 111-148, as amended) included a provision to impose an excise tax on high-cost employer-sponsored insurance (ESI) coverage beginning in 2018. This provision, popularly termed the *Cadillac tax*, imposes an excise tax on ESI coverage in excess of a predetermined threshold. The tax is imposed on the coverage provider, typically the health insurance provider or the entity that administers the plan benefits.

Currently, employers' spending on ESI coverage and most employees' contributions to ESI plans are exempt from income and payroll taxes. Although proposals to limit the amount of health insurance benefits eligible for this exclusion were considered, the ACA, as enacted, did not limit the exclusion for employer-provided health insurance

* This is an edited, reformatted and augmented version of a Congressional Research Service publication R44159, prepared for Members and Committees of Congress, dated August 20, 2015.

coverage. The Cadillac tax discourages high-cost employer health plans through another approach.

The Cadillac tax is imposed at a rate of 40%. This tax rate is applied on a *tax-exclusive basis*, as is generally the case with excise tax rates. That is, like a sales tax, the rate applies to the price or cost excluding the tax. By contrast, the tax rate relevant to an income tax exclusion is on a *tax-inclusive basis*: it is applied to a base that includes the tax. The Cadillac tax is nondeductible from the insurer's gross income (or the employer's gross income, in cases where the employer self-insures). This treatment is unlike other excise taxes.

The Cadillac tax takes effect in 2018 and is imposed on plans that cost more than $10,200 for single health plans and $27,500 for non-single (e.g., family) plans. The exempt amount is indexed for inflation, and, because health costs tend to grow faster than inflation, the share of premiums covered by the tax and the revenue collected is expected to grow.

This report examines several issues. It evaluates the potential of the Cadillac tax to affect health insurance coverage and the health care market. It also examines the expected incidence (burden) of the tax—that is, which group's income will be reduced by the tax. Finally, the report discusses implications for economic efficiency in the context of tax administration.

Estimates suggest that the Cadillac tax could lead to an overall decline in the quantity of health services as some firms reduce the size of their insurance coverage. This decline is estimated to range from 0.5% to 0.6% in 2018 and from 2.2% to 2.5% in 2024. Prices could fall by up to 0.4% in 2018 and up to 1.5% in 2024 (although costs paid by some consumers could rise due to cutbacks in Cadillac plans). Overall expenditure (the sum of the fall in quantity and the fall in price) could decline by 0.6%-0.9% in 2018 and by 2.5%-3.6% in 2024. In other words, the tax could result in a gross reduction of $7.6-$11.0 billion in national health expenditures in 2018 and $41.0-$60.3 billion by 2024.

Although the tax is imposed on insurers or employers, the burden is expected to fall on wages. In some cases, employers will retain the Cadillac insurance plans and pass the tax on to workers in the form of lower wages. In other cases, employers will substitute taxable wages for insurance coverage in excess of the threshold, and employees will be subject to income and payroll taxes on those wages. Revenue projections assume the latter situation will be more common.

INTRODUCTION

Employer health care plans benefit from the ability to exclude the value of the insurance paid by the employer from employee income and payroll taxes. This provision, known as the employer-sponsored insurance (ESI) tax exclusion, has been viewed by some as encouraging too much spending on insurance and therefore on health care. During consideration of the Patient Protection and Affordable Care Act (ACA; P.L. 111-148, as amended) proposals to limit the amount of benefit excluded from tax under this provision were addressed.[1]

The final bill did not limit the amount of benefits employees can exclude from income and payroll taxes, but it did include a related provision that is popularly termed the *Cadillac tax*. This provision imposes an excise tax on the cost of ESI coverage that is in excess of a predetermined threshold. The Cadillac tax differs from other typical excise taxes in two ways: it is imposed on amounts in excess of a dollar floor, and it is not deductible from the income tax. It is imposed on the coverage provider, either a third-party insurer or, in the case of self-financed plans, the plan administrator (which may be the employer).

The Cadillac tax is imposed at a rate of 40%. This tax rate is applied on a *tax-exclusive basis*, as is generally the case with excise tax rates. That is, like a sales tax, it applies to the price or cost excluding the tax. By contrast, the tax rate relevant to an income tax exclusion is on a *tax-inclusive basis*: it is applied to a base that includes the tax. A 40% tax applied on a tax-exclusive basis is equivalent to a 28.57% rate (0.4/1.4) applied on a tax-inclusive basis. That is, if the tax base is $100 dollars, the tax will add $40. The rate on a tax-inclusive basis is the tax ($40) divided by the base plus the tax ($140). The Cadillac tax is nondeductible from the insurer's gross income (or the employer's gross income, in cases where the employer self-insures). This treatment is unlike other excise taxes. (See the *Appendix* for further discussion).

The Cadillac tax takes effect in 2018 and is imposed on plans that cost more than $10,200 for single health plans and $27,500 for non-single (e.g., family) plans. The exempt amount is indexed for inflation, and, because health costs tend to grow faster than inflation, the share of premiums covered by the tax and the revenue collected is expected to grow over time.[2]

Unlike a limit on the exclusion of benefits, which would increase the taxable income of the employee, this tax is imposed on the coverage provider, often the health insurer. Like the proposals to amend the employer health care exclusion that were discussed before the tax was adopted, however, the Cadillac tax is aimed not only at providing financial support for the costs of the ACA (such as premium subsidies to help lower-income individuals purchase health insurance) but also at reducing expenditures on health care.

This report examines several issues. It evaluates the potential of the Cadillac tax to affect health insurance coverage and, therefore, the health market. It also examines the expected incidence (burden) of the tax—that is, which group will pay the price of the tax. In addition, the report discusses the efficiency of the tax in the context of administrative cost.

ECONOMIC EFFICIENCY AND THE HEALTH INSURANCE AND HEALTH CARE MARKET

The health care sector contains many sources of market failure, which create economic inefficiencies.[3] The inefficiency that is most directly related to the Cadillac tax is the moral-hazard issue that results from having health insurance. In general, insured individuals spend more on medical care than they would without insurance. More demand for medical care raises the price of medical care, and it could reduce incentives for individuals to take responsibility for their health status (to the extent that they can).[4] Incentives that encourage insurance consumption, such as the unlimited ESI tax exclusion, can increase these inefficiencies in the market for medical care. The Cadillac tax is intended in part to reduce this source of inefficiency. Although some employers and employees may choose to retain high-cost plans, others may scale back to avoid the tax. For employees in the latter group, the cost of health care increases, for example, through higher co-payments and larger deductibles.

A Graphical Depiction of the Health Care Market

Figure 1 illustrates the effects of the Cadillac tax on the national market for medical care using a supply and demand framework. In this diagram, the effects of insurance and the Cadillac tax are depicted as the share of cost, s, paid by insurance. Therefore, the cost to the consumer is P(1-s), where P is the market price of the health care.

Note also that the points on the graph do not reflect magnitudes but are illustrative, as the effect of the Cadillac tax is small relative to the effect of insurance.[5]

The points on the graph can be defined as follows:

- P* and Q* are the price and quantity in a market without insurance, where consumers face the full costs of their medical care decisions.
- Pi and Qi are the price and quantity in a market with insurance and subsidies (such as the ESI tax exclusion), where individual consumers pay a portion of their medical costs out of pocket at the price Pi(1-si).
- Pt and Qt are the price and quantity in a market with insurance and subsidies, where individual consumers face a higher price because insurance coverage has been reduced by the Cadillac tax, where individual consumers pay Pt(1-sj.

The demand curve is steeply sloped downward, indicating the demand for medical care is relatively inelastic, or changes in quantity demanded are relatively insensitive to changes in price.[6] The supply curve is gradually upward sloping, indicating that the supply of medical care services is relatively elastic, or changes in the quantity supplied are relatively responsive to changes in price.[7]

In a world without insurance, consumers pay the full price of medical care (P*) and demand an amount of medical care (Q*) at the intersection of supply and demand. In a world where insurance is introduced, individual consumers pay a share of their full medical costs, $P(1\text{-}s_i)$, in the form of a co-payment or other cost sharing and demand Q_i amount of medical care. Prices (or cost per unit) in the medical care market increase from P* to P_i after the introduction of insurance as suppliers capture a portion of the subsidy.

Equilibrium in the medical care market after introduction of insurance occurs with price P_i and quantity Q_i. In other words, consumers tend to demand a greater quantity of medical care in a world with health insurance compared to a world without health insurance because insured individuals face a lower out-of-pocket cost, $P_i(1\text{-}s_i)$ as compared to P*. The ESI tax exclusion intensifies the effects that insurance has on the quantity demanded and the prevailing price of medical care in the market because it further insulates consumers from the full price of their medical care decisions.

The Cadillac tax effectively reduces (or offsets) federal subsidies for health insurance and reduces that insurance coverage.

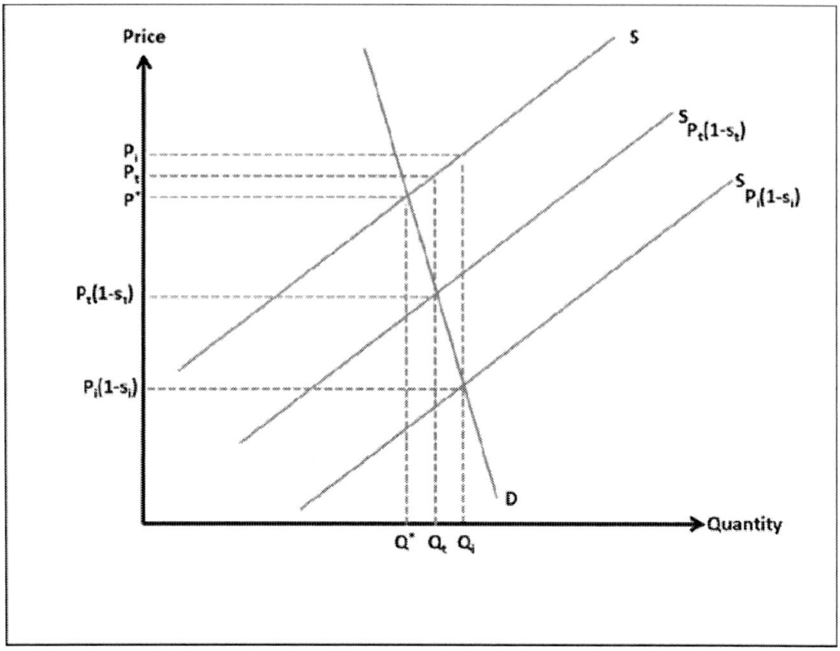

Source: CRS analysis, informed by select, empirical findings of elasticities of supply and demand.

Notes: The tax has effects on only part of the population, and this graph depicts an aggregated effect.

P* and Q* are the price and quantity in a market without insurance, where consumers face the full costs of their medical decisions.

Pi and Qi are the price and quantity in a market with insurance and subsidies (such as the employer-sponsored health insurance tax exclusion), where individual consumers pay a portion of their medical costs out of pocket at the price Pi(1-si).

Pt and Qt are the price and quantity in a market with insurance and subsidies, where individual consumers face a higher price because insurance coverage has been reduced by the Cadillac tax.

The symbols st and si refer to the share paid by insurance with and without the Cadillac tax.

Figure 1. Supply and Demand Effects of the Cadillac Tax.

Thus, it increases consumers' exposure to the full cost of their medical care beyond the Cadillac-tax threshold such that the total quantity of medical care demanded decreases from Q_i to Q_t and price decreases from P_i to P_t. The equilibrium after imposition of the Cadillac tax is closer to the equilibrium in the market without the effects of health insurance. The decline in quantity from Q_i to Q_t largely represents sensitivity to higher out-of-pocket costs (in the form of higher co-payments, deductibles, or other features).

Estimated Effects of the Tax on Health Care Prices and Quantities

The Cadillac tax will affect the overall medical care market by effectively reducing government subsidies for health insurance and therefore reducing insurance coverage, which would likely lead to an increased cost of medical care for the consumer. As medical care becomes more costly, spending on medical care will decrease and spending on other commodities will increase.

While the theoretical prediction is that the Cadillac tax will reduce medical care spending, the revenue raised by the tax is estimated to be a small share of national health expenditures. According to the Congressional Budget Office, the tax will raise $3 billion in revenue in 2018 and $17 billion in 2024.[8] The Centers for Medicare & Medicaid Services (CMS) project that national health care expenditures will be $1.259 trillion in 2018 and $1.746 trillion in 2024.[9] In other words, revenue raised by the Cadillac tax is projected to amount to 0.2% of projected national health expenditures in 2018 and 1.0% in 2024.[10] Although the tax is small relative to health spending, its effects can be multiplied through reductions in insurance coverage, as discussed below.

Once the tax is implemented, some firms (on behalf of their workers) will retain their plans and pay the tax. Other firms will reduce their insurance and pay their employees more, so that revenue gains will reflect the increase in income and payroll tax paid on the increase in taxable compensation.[11] These additional wages would substitute for previously untaxed health benefits. The reduced insurance coverage would be a multiple of the tax revenues. For example, if the tax rate is 30%, each $30 of revenue collected equals $100 of taxable income and reduced coverage. Thus, each dollar of revenue reflects $3.33 ($100/$30) of reduced coverage. Based on estimates shown in the *Appendix* that apply assumptions used by the Joint Committee on Taxation, more than three-quarters of premiums above the Cadillac-tax threshold could be eliminated and replaced by wages. This reduction in coverage would increase the cost of health care to those formerly covered by a Cadillac plan. While there are a number of ways in which costs could be reduced in an insurance policy, the analysis here assumes a proportional effect on the share paid by the individual consumer.[12]

After incorporating the elasticities of demand and supply mentioned above, the Cadillac tax could lead to an overall decline in the quantity of health services. This decline is estimated to range from 0.5% to 0.6% of health services in 2018 and from 2.2% to 2.5% in 2024. Prices could fall by up to 0.4% in 2018 and up to 1.5% in 2024, although costs to some consumers would increase as the Cadillac tax reduced the subsidy for health insurance. Overall expenditure (the sum of the fall in quantity and the fall in price) could decline by 0.6%-0.9% in 2018 and by 2.5%-3.6% in 2024.[13] In other words, the tax could result in a gross reduction of $7.6-$11.2 billion in national health expenditures in 2018 and $41.0-$60.3 billion by 2024, based on the same CMS baseline projections of health spending mentioned above.[14]

Effects on Wages

The Cadillac tax is expected to decrease after-tax compensation. These effects are expected to occur regardless of whether revenue is collected from the Cadillac tax or firms change health insurance offerings in response to the tax.

Some employers might choose to maintain health plans that are subject to the Cadillac tax. In this case, third-party insurers could pass along the direct cost of the tax as well as any other indirect markups in the price of the premiums to consumers to offset the insurers' higher income tax liabilities. The higher income tax liability for the third-party insurer arises because the Cadillac tax increases the price of insurance, which increases revenue and, in turn, increases income tax payments.[15] This *feedback effect* from the tax is due to the fact that the Cadillac tax is, by statute, nondeductible to the third-party insurer. Employers are likely to pass these added costs to employees by reducing wages. Similarly, self-insured employers, who are directly responsible for paying the Cadillac tax, would likely pass along any added costs to workers in the form of lower wages. As shown in the *Appendix*, both the Cadillac tax and the increased income tax should be considered add-ons to the base (or tax exclusive). Also, as shown in the *Appendix*, the tax effects (which include Cadillac tax, income tax from nondeductibility, and employer payroll tax effects) if translated into a comparable tax-inclusive rate applied to the employee would be equivalent to an exclusion at a tax rate of 35% (combined payroll tax and income tax).

Alternatively, employers might respond by reducing insurance coverage and raising employees' wages. These higher wages would be subject to income and payroll taxes. Since the Cadillac tax is equivalent to a 35% exclusion, its burden is higher when the combined tax rate is below that level. Thus, reducing insurance coverage would increase after-tax wages for some employees as compared to retaining the tax. Either way, the burden would be expected to fall on wages since the tax is an increase in the cost of compensation.[16]

The lower effective earnings in sectors most affected by the Cadillac tax could lead employees to move to other jobs. The increased supply of workers seeking jobs could drive down wages. This scenario, however, is likely to be small because workers would only face a tax on the portion of their health benefits above the Cadillac tax threshold. With this said, the burden of the tax would be expected to fall on wages as long as the overall supply of labor is relatively fixed, with an accompanying shift of labor and production out of the affected sectors into other sectors.[17] The extent to which the burden is spread beyond those firms depends on a complex mix of substitutability among products and production processes.

The analysis above reflects the *long-term* effects on labor markets. In the short run, wages are sometimes "sticky" and bound by the terms of particular contracts or labor agreements. Indeed, some industries that have rigid labor contracts might be slower to adjust than others (although the Cadillac tax was enacted in 2010, eight years in advance of its 2018 implementation date).

EFFECTS ON SOCIAL WELFARE AND ADMINISTRATIVE COSTS

The analysis of the effects of the Cadillac tax cannot determine whether the tax results in a net increase or decrease in social welfare and therefore an efficiency gain. The health care sector is host to a number of phenomena that either increase or decrease social well-being. The Cadillac tax reduces the moral-hazard inefficiencies associated with insurance (thereby increasing social well-being). However, the efficiency gain is reduced by the tax's administrative and compliance costs. In addition, by making insurance more expensive for some individuals, the Cadillac tax could also erode, over time, some of the benefit derived from the social-insurance function of lifetime medical-expense cost sharing. In the current health care system, the young and healthy subsidize health care costs for the elderly and less healthy, and those with greater abilities to pay insurance premiums subsidize costs for those who might be unable to pay for health care. As the Cadillac tax increases its coverage over time, a larger share of employer premiums will be affected.[18]

The Cadillac tax, however, is likely easier to administer than the alternative of taxing insurance benefits above a base. A major economic issue impeding the taxation of employer-sponsored health care benefits is measuring the imputed value of health benefits received. Some measures of a health plan's value are now available on an employee's W-2 form, but this amount could be closer to an average cost per worker across an employer's workforce and does not necessarily represent the value of health benefits received by the particular taxpayer.[19]

APPENDIX. ESTIMATING THE EFFECTS OF THE TAX ON HEALTH MARKETS AND WAGES

Deriving the Effects of the Cadillac Tax on Price and Quantity in the Medical Care Market

The effects of the Cadillac tax on the medical care market can be expressed as a percentage change in price and quantity.

First, the demand equation, with values subscripted with D, can be specified as

$$QD = AD[P(1\text{-}s)]\text{\^{}}ED \qquad (1)$$

where QD is the quantity of medical care demanded, AD is a constant, P is price, s is the share of medical costs paid by the insurer, and ED is the absolute value of the elasticity of demand.

The supply equation, with values subscripted by S, can be specified as

$$QS = ASP\text{\^{}}ES \qquad (2)$$

where AS is a constant, P is price, and ES is the elasticity of supply.

Next, equations (1) and (2) can be transformed into percentage changes in quantity demanded and quantity supplied, using natural logarithms:

$$\ln QD = -ED[\ln P + \ln(1\text{-}s)] \qquad (3)$$

and

$$\ln Q_S = E_S(\ln P) \quad (4)$$

Then, equations (3) and (4) can be equated and differentiated and the percentage change in price (P′) can be expressed as

$$P' = [E_D/(E_D+E_S)]*[-ds/(1-s)] \quad (5)$$

Here, ds is the change in the size of the subsidy (which decreases). The percentage change in quantity (Q′) can be expressed as

$$Q' = P'*E_S \quad (6)$$

Remember that (1-s) = share of health care costs paid by the insurer. In our calculations, $E_D = 0.2$, $(1\text{-}s) = 0.19$, and $E_S = 1.5$ or infinity. The estimation of that value requires further analysis and is reported in the final section of this Appendix.

Effects of the Tax on Wages

The Cadillac tax will be applied as a tax-exclusive rate and imposed at a rate of 40%. Internal Revenue Code Section 4980I(d)(2)(A) states that the cost of coverage does not include the "cost attributable to the tax," which presumably means the tax itself (and presumably the increased income taxes due to the lack of deductibility) should be eliminated from the tax base.

A key issue is whether a tax rate is stated on a tax-exclusive or tax-inclusive basis. A tax rate stated on a tax-exclusive basis is a rate applied to the cost before the application of the tax, as in the case of a sales tax. A tax rate stated on a tax-inclusive basis, as in the case of an income tax, would be much smaller. The statute seems to indicate that tax itself should not be included in the base (i.e., on a tax-exclusive basis), but the wording is somewhat ambiguous with respect to increased income taxes. A recent Internal Revenue Service (IRS) notice clarifies the treatment, which is consistent with the discussion in this section.[20] Ignoring the issue of a lack of deduction from the income tax, the tax-exclusive rate should be 28.57% (0.4 divided by 1.4) of the employer-sponsored insurance (ESI) benefit above the threshold charged by a third-party provider. That is, if $40 is paid on $100 of charges before the tax is imposed, \$40 will be 28.57% of the total sales price of \$140 including the tax. The lack of income-tax deductibility complicates this simple formulation, as discussed below, and indicates that for a third-party provider subject to the 35% income tax rate, the tax rate would be 24.76% to account for the additional income tax due and the higher price it produces.

The following sections discuss how the regulation would need to be implemented (which is how it appears to have been outlined in the recent IRS notice) to equate the treatment of self-insured plans and plans contracted with third-party insurers. They also explain how the 40% rate on excess health benefits and the lack of income tax deductibility make for an effective deterrent for most consumers to take up high-cost health plans. In addition, the following sections estimate the price markup that insurance companies would have to charge as premiums on excess benefits and provide some of the data needed to estimate the effects on health care spending.

First, the effects of the Cadillac tax are derived for a self-insured company, which directly administers its employees' health plans. According to surveys, 61% of workers covered by employer-sponsored plans are in plans that are fully or partially self-funded by their employer.[21] Second, the example of the self-insured company will be used to inform the effects of the tax on a third-party insurance company and the measure of tax. As shown in the following calculations, self-insured firms pay the Cadillac tax based on their calculations of health benefits that exceed the Cadillac-tax threshold, and it is not necessary to charge a price for insurance. In contrast, third-party insurers can increase the price of their plans to compensate for any excise or income tax payments. Although the transmission mechanism of the economic burden of the Cadillac tax might be different in these two cases, the ultimate effects are equivalent: employees bear the economic burden of the Cadillac tax in the form of lower wages (for those that retain plans subject to the Cadillac tax) or taxes on the increase in taxable compensation (for those that forgo plans subject to the Cadillac tax). All of the calculations in this section assume that the tax is administered on a tax-exclusive basis, that the burden of the tax falls on labor, and that other costs and profits remain fixed.

Self-Insured Firms

A firm's total revenue (TR), cost (TC), and profit conditions (it) can be expressed as

$$(TR\text{-}TC) = it \qquad (7)$$

Total costs can be decomposed into wages (W), other costs (C), and excess Cadillac benefits (B) (with Cadillac benefits determined as medical payments in excess of medical costs above the Cadillac ceiling). Taxes are levied on income at rate t. Before imposition of the Cadillac tax, with p the rate for the employer's share of the payroll tax, equation (2) relates total revenue minus total cost divided in its components and subjected to an income tax at rate t:

$$[TR-W(1+p)-C-B](1-t) = it(1-t), \text{ and solving for } W \quad (8)$$

$$W = (TR-C-B-it)/(1+p) \quad (9)$$

with the imposition of the tax at a 0.4 rate and no deductibility,

$$[TR-W(1+p)-C-B*1.4]-t[TR-W(1+p)-C-B] = it(1-t) \quad (10)$$

$$W= [TR-C-B-it -0.4B/(1-t)]/(1+p) \quad (11)$$

Therefore, subtracting (9) from (11), the change in W, dW, is

$$dW = -0.4B/[(1-t)(1+p)] \quad (12)$$

The change in W for a nonprofit or government employer not subject to tax would be 0.4B/(1+p), so these plans are favored.

The taxes can now be divided into the following components. First, the firm pays 0.4B as a Cadillac tax. The firm also pays a corporate tax on the increase in profits of dW, which is t0.4B/[(1-t)(1+p)]. Since wages have decreased, the firm decreases its payroll tax by -p(1- t)0.4B/[(1-t)(1+p)]. Finally, the employee pays reduced employee payroll and income tax at a combined rate, t, on the fall in wages, or (0.4B)(t)/[(1-t)(1+p)]. Based on estimates that the combined individual rate (individual income taxes and the employee's share of the payroll tax) is approximately 30%, t is 0.35, and p is 0.0765, the corporate and individual income tax revenue terms sum to zero, leaving only the Cadillac tax of 40% on the original excess benefit. The individual loss in after-tax wage, the fall in wage minus the tax reductions on the fall in wages 0.4B/[(1-t)- 0.4B(t)]/[(1-t)(1+p)] is 0.4B.

This analysis also indicates that whenever the combined individual tax rate is greater than 35%, a lower tax is paid by keeping the Cadillac tax and paying the tax rather than giving up the benefits and taking the excess in taxable wages. Since wages rise, the firm will have to pay higher payroll taxes, so that the change in wages times (1+p) is equal to B, or the increase in wages is B/(1+p). The firm pays a payroll tax of pB/(1+p), and the worker pays a tax of tB/(1+p). The sum of taxes is (p+t)B/(1+p). Collecting the term for taxes paid under the Cadillac tax when benefits are retained, they are 0.4B(1-t)/[(1-u)(1+p)]. When the tax rate, t, including a 7.65% employee payroll tax, is greater than 35% (implying an income tax rate of 28%), it would be cheaper to pay the tax.[22] Thus, both the high rate and the lack of income tax deductibility help to make the Cadillac tax effective in eliminating demand for most excess health benefits, which is the objective of the tax.

Third-Party Insurer: How Insurance Firms Incorporate the Tax in the Price for Health Benefits

There has been debate and speculation over how much insurers could mark up plans subject to the Cadillac tax.

Returning to equation (7), now treat total revenue as PQ, where P is price and Q is quantity and total cost is CQ+B. It is simpler to express amounts B and it as per unit of output since this is a per-unit calculation, then Q = 1.

The per-unit profit equation for an insurance firm in a world without the 40% Cadillac tax is

$$(P-C-B)(1-\mu) = it(1-\mu), \text{ and } P = C + B + it \tag{13}$$

The profit equation in a world with the 40% Cadillac tax imposed on the original excess benefit (assuming the tax is not deductible) can be set up, with P* the price before the Cadillac tax, as

$$(P^*-C-1.4B)-\mu(1.4P^*-C) = it(1-\mu) \tag{14}$$

$$P^* = C + B + it + 0.4B/(1-\mu) \tag{15}$$

Since P (the original price) can be substituted for the equation C+B+it, the percentage change in price is 0.4/(1-μ) times the excess benefit per unit, or 61.536% times the original excess benefit base. Out of that increase, 40% is paid in a tax and 35% of the revenue increase (21.536%) is paid in corporate income tax. Therefore, if the only information is how much the insurance premium exceeds the base, the excise that should be levied on that premium is 0.4/[1+0.4/(1-μ)] or 24.76%, rather than the standard excise tax conversion rate of 28.57% (0.4/1.4).

If this rule is followed, and the additional price passed on to wages, the same results will occur for self-insured firms and third-party insurers. There will be no effect on the employer because the higher cost of insurance will be offset by reductions in cost due to wages. Tax-exempt employers are no different from taxable ones. The employer will reduce the wage bill, W(1+p), by the increase in price, 0.4B/(1-μ). The employer will pay 0.4B(p)/[(1-u)(1+p)], and the individual will pay a tax of 0.4B(t)/[(1-μ)(1+p)]. The sum of the taxes paid by the all the parties is 0.4B(1-t)/[(1-μ)(1+p)].

However, if a third-party insurer is tax exempt, the appropriate effective tax is 28.57% and the price increase is 0.4. That is, both tax-exempt self-insured plans and tax-exempt third-party insurers receive favorable treatment because of the lack of deductibility of the tax.

Estimates

To complete the estimates, the revenue estimates from the Joint Committee on Taxation (JCT) are used to estimate the change in the size of the subsidy (ds). JCT has indicated that a quarter of the revenues are from Cadillac tax collections (which would be the amount paid on plans that are kept) and the remainder are from income taxes on plans that were eliminated. If x is the share of plans kept, then 0.4x/[(p+t)(1-x)/(1+p)] = 1/3. In that case, 21.31% of the benefits are kept and the remainder, 78.69%, are eliminated and replaced by wages. In addition, each dollar of revenue is only the tax, and the associated benefit is (1+0.0765)/0.35[23] [(1+p)/(p+t)] or 3.075. Thus, the aggregate change in subsidy is 0.787 times 3.075 times the total revenue gain. This gain ($3 billion in 2018 and $17 billion in 2024) is divided by total health spending ($1.259 trillion in 2018 and $1.746 trillion in 2024) to convert to a percentage. Note that the share of reduced benefits would be slightly smaller if nonprofit self-insurers and nonprofit third-party insurers were taken into account and the resulting effects on the aggregate market would be slightly larger.

Table A-1 and *Table A-2* provide the assumptions and results of the calculations.

Table A-1. Assumptions for Calculations Related to the Cadillac Tax

Assumption	Value
Elasticity of Demand (ED), Absolute Value	0.2
Low Elasticity of Supply (ES)	1.5
High Elasticity of Supply (ES)	infinity
Initial Share of Costs Paid by Consumer (1-s)	0.19
Share of Plans Eliminated	0.787
Payroll Tax Rate, Employer (p)	0.0765
Sum of Employee Payroll Tax and Income Tax	0.35
Loss of Benefit Per Dollar of Revenue	3.075
Revenue Divided by Health Spending, 2018 (%)	0.238
Revenue Divided by Health Spending, 20.24 (%)	0.974

Source: Congressional Research Service, see text.

Table A-2. Estimated Effects of the Cadillac Tax on Price, Quantity and Spending in the Medical Care Market: Results of Calculations

Year/ES Assumption	Fall in Price (%)	Fall in Quantity (%)	Fall in Spending (%)
2018			
Low	0.36	0.54	0.89
High	0.00	0.61	0.61
2024			
Low	1.46	2.19	3.65
High	0.00	2.48	2.48

Source: Congressional Research Service, see text.

End Notes

[1] U.S. Congress, Senate Committee on Finance, Description of Policy Options: Financing Comprehensive Health Care Reform: Proposed Health System Savings and Revenue Options, May 20, 2009, at http://www.finance.senate.gov/ newsroom/ranking/download/?id=8a3deecc-59d2-4530-ba0e-8862a05ed714.

[2] For an overview of the Cadillac tax see CRS Report R44147, Excise Tax on High-Cost Employer-Sponsored Health Coverage: In Brief, by Annie L. Mach. For a more detailed history and an analysis of the growth in coverage of the tax, see CRS Report R44160, The Excise Tax on High-Cost Employer-Sponsored Health Coverage: Background and Economic Analysis, by Sean Lowry.

[3] Some of these inefficiencies are summarized in Joseph Stiglitz, Economics of the Public Sector, 3rd ed. (New York: Norton), pp. 300-330; and Executive Office of the President, Council of Economic Advisers, The Economic Case for Health Care Reform, June 2009, pp. 9-17, at https://www.whitehouse.gov/assets/documents/ CEA_Health_Care_Report.pdf.

[4] Joseph Stiglitz, Economics of the Public Sector, 3rd ed. (New York: Norton), p. 315.

[5] Supply and demand curves are depicted as straight lines in the graph for illustrative purposes, although in the estimates of quantitative effects, demand, and supply are treated as constant elastic functions.

[6] An elasticity of demand for insured health services of -0.2 is commonly referred to in the health economics literature. For example, see Su Liu and Deborah Chollet, Price and Income Elasticity of the Demand for Health Insurance and Health Care Services: A Critical Review of the Literature, Mathematica Policy Research, Inc., March 24, 2006, at http://www.mathematica-mpr.com/publications/pdfs/priceincome.pdf. Although some economists caution the use of a single elasticity to describe all medical spending, studies of different types of medical care often find demand to still be relatively inelastic (i.e., less than 1.0 in absolute-value terms). See Avira Aron-Dine, Liran Einav, and Amy Finkelstein, "The RAND Health Insurance Experiment, Three Decades Later," Journal of Economic Perspectives, vol. 27, no. 1 (Winter 2013), pp. 197-222, at http://economics.mit.edu/files/8400; and Sherman Folland, Allen C. Goodman, and Miron Stano, The Economics of Health and Health Care, 6th ed. (Upper Saddle River, NJ: Prentice Hall, 2010), p. 179.

[7] Various researchers have studied the price elasticity of supply, with regard to various categories of health care services, with the consensus being that the supply curve is positively sloped with an elasticity much greater than 1.0. The supply curve in Figure 1 approximates an elasticity of 1.5 for physician services for Medicare Part B found in Jeffrey Clemens and Joshua D. Gottlieb, "Do Physician's Financial Incentives Affect Medical Treatment and Patient Health?," American Economic Review, vol. 104, no. 4 (April 2014), pp. 1320-1349. Previous studies of physician payments find similar results. For example, see Jack Hadley et al., "Medicare Fees and the Volume of Physicians' Services," Inquiry, vol. 46, no. 4 (Winter 2009), pp. 372-390. Other studies find that financial incentives strongly affect the development and production of pharmaceuticals, an input into health service provision. For example, see Daron Acemoglu and Joshua Linn, "Market Size in Innovation: Theory and Evidence from the Pharmaceutical Industry," Quarterly Journal of Economics, vol. 119, no. 3 (2004), pp. 1040-1090; and Ali Yurukoglu, Medicare Reimbursements and Shortages of Sterile Injectable Pharmaceuticals, National Bureau of Economic Research (NBER), NBER Working Paper No. 17987, April 2012, at http://www.nber.org/papers/w17987. This 1.5 elasticity represents only physician's services including labor supply and investment in offices; there are many other inputs into health care that are likely to be supplied in increased amounts at the same price because they are goods made with constant returns to scale (e.g., hospital buildings, medical equipment and supplies in hospital and other health institution settings, drugs), producing an infinite supply elasticity. The response of other health professionals such as nurses, technicians, and nursing assistants may also be more elastic than that of physicians. Because the overall elasticity of health care is likely to be larger than 1.5, the calculations in this report present a range between two supply elasticity assumptions: 1.5 and infinity.

[8] Congressional Budget Office (CBO), Budgetary and Economic Effects of Repealing the Affordable Care Act, June 2015, at https://www.cbo.gov/sites/default/files/114th-congress-2015-2016/reports/50252- Effects_of_ACA_Repeal_0.pdf.

[9] See Centers for Medicare & Medicaid Services (CMS), National Health Expenditures Projections, "NHE Projections 2014-2024 – Tables," July 30, 2015, at https://www.cms.gov/Research-Statistics-Data-and-Systems/Statistics-Trendsand-Reports/National HealthExpendData/NationalHealthAccountsProjected.html. CMS also project "personal

health care expenditure" (which is equal to health care expenditures minus research, structures, equipment, net cost of health insurance, and government public health activities) of $1.105 trillion in 2018 and $1.537 trillion in 2024.

[10] If replicated for shares of "personal health care expenditures," these calculations would be less than 1% in 2018 and 1.1% in 2024.

[11] See discussion in the "Effects on Wages" section.

[12] A policy could increase co-payments, limit the scope of coverage, limit the network of preferred providers, decrease deductibles, or limit catastrophic coverage. All of these would in some way change spending on medical care.

[13] The ranges reflect a demand elasticity of -0.2 and supply elasticities set at 1.5 and at infinity. Formulas for these calculations are shown in the Appendix. The analysis relies on revenue estimates from the Joint Committee on Taxation (JCT) to determine the share of plans affected and the size of the change in health costs. The effect on price is zero for an infinitely elastic supply curve, but price falls with a 1.5 supply elasticity. Reductions in quantity are larger for an infinite elasticity than for the 1.5 elasticity. The effect on health expenditures, capturing both the fall in price and the fall in quantity, is larger for the 1.5 elasticity.

[14] As consumers affected by the Cadillac tax decrease their medical care consumption in response to the tax, consumers not affected by the Cadillac tax could increase their consumption slightly (estimated at no more than 0.2%) and partially offset the effects of the tax. Still, the decline in consumption by those affected exceeds the increase in consumption by those not affected.

[15] This analysis assumes that the insurance market is competitive and that insurance companies will need to pass any additional costs forward to remain in the market.

[16] This is a standard view of a tax that burdens employee compensation. In its 2009 distributional analysis of a previous version of the Cadillac tax, JCT appeared to largely assume that the insurer would pass the full price of the tax along to the consumer and that employers would largely pass any increase in costs to wages. See Letter from Thomas A. Barthold, Chief of Staff, Joint Committee on Taxation, to the Hon. Joe Courtney, U.S. House of Representatives, October 16, 2009, p. 2. This assumption was reaffirmed in CBO, Updated Estimates of the Effects of the Insurance Coverage Provisions of the Affordable Care Act, April 2014, p. 13, at https://www.cbo.gov/publication/45231. It was also the position taken by Gordon Mermim and Eric Toder, Analysis of Bipartisan Policy Center Cadillac Tax Replacement Option, Tax Policy Center, July 2015, at http://taxpolicycenter.org/UploadedPDF/2000310-bpc-cadillacreplacement-tax.pdf.

[17] If the tax fell uniformly on all workers, it would be expected to fall on wages without other significant consequences since the supply of labor is relatively inelastic. In this case, the tax is imposed on some workers and not others, making it a partial-factor tax that could be shifted to other workers. It is similar to the effects of a partial-factor tax on capital as shown in Arnold Harberger, "The Incidence of the Corporate Income Tax," Journal of Political Economy, vol. 70, June 1962, pp. 215-240.

[18] See CRS Report R44160, The Excise Tax on High-Cost Employer-Sponsored Health Coverage: Background and Economic Analysis, by Sean Lowry, for estimates of the share of premiums covered over time.

[19] For a discussion of the problems associated with imputing income from employer health benefits, see Stan Dorn, Capping the Tax Exclusion of Employer-Sponsored Health Insurance: Is Equity Feasible?, June 2009, at http://www.urban.org/sites/ default/files/

alfresco/publication-pdfs/411894-Capping-the-Tax-Exclusion-of-EmployerSponsored-Health-Insurance-Is-Equity-Feasible-.PDF.

[20] See Internal Revenue Code §4980I(d)(2)(A): "The cost of applicable employer-sponsored coverage shall be determined under rules similar to the rules of section 4980B(f)(4), except that in determining such cost, any portion of the cost of such coverage which is attributable to the tax imposed under this section shall not be taken into account and the amount of such cost shall be calculated separately for self-only coverage and other coverage." A recent notice, Internal Revenue Service (IRS) Notice 2015-52, indicates the same treatment as derived in this analysis. See IRS Notice 2015-52, issued July 30, 2015, at http://www.irs.gov/pub/irs-drop/n-15-52.pdf.

[21] Exhibit 10.1 in Kaiser Family Foundation (KFF), 2014 Annual Survey of Employer Health Benefits, September 10, 2014, at http://kff.org/health-costs/report/2014-employer-health-benefits-survey/.

[22] If incomes are high enough to exceed the Social Security payroll tax ceiling (currently $118,500), the payroll tax is only the Medicare tax of 1.45% and the tax rate would have to exceed 37%. Very high-income individuals have to pay an additional employee tax of 0.9%, which would make the rate slightly lower.

[23] This value is (1+p)/(p+t) as derived in the previous section.

In: The "Cadillac" Tax on Employer Health Plans ISBN: 978-1-63484-246-4
Editor: Leslie Caldwell

Chapter 3

EXCISE TAX ON HIGH-COST EMPLOYER-SPONSORED HEALTH COVERAGE: IN BRIEF*

Annie L. Mach

SUMMARY

The Patient Protection and Affordable Care Act (ACA; P.L. 111-148, as amended) includes a 40% excise tax on high-cost employer-sponsored health coverage. This tax, often called the *Cadillac tax*, is to be implemented beginning in 2018.

The excise tax was included in the ACA to raise revenue to offset the cost of other ACA provisions. According to the Congressional Budget Office and the Joint Committee on Taxation, the excise tax is expected to increase federal revenues by $87 billion between 2016 and 2025.

The excise tax applies to the aggregate cost of an employee's applicable coverage that exceeds a dollar limit. Applicable coverage includes, but is not limited to, the employer's and the employee's contribution to health insurance premiums and certain contributions to tax-advantaged health accounts (e.g., health care flexible spending accounts, or FSAs).

In 2018, the dollar limits are $10,200 for single coverage and $27,500 for non-single (e.g., family) coverage. The dollar limits may be adjusted based on growth in health insurance premiums and

* This is an edited, reformatted and augmented version of a Congressional Research Service publication R44147, prepared for Members and Committees of Congress, dated August 14, 2015.

characteristics of an employer's workforce. Additionally, the dollar limits are to be adjusted for inflation in subsequent years.

The entity providing the coverage, the coverage provider, is responsible for paying its share of the excise tax. A coverage provider may be an employer, a health insurer, or another entity that sponsors the coverage. The employer is responsible for calculating the amount of tax owed by each coverage provider (if any).

All of this information is covered in more detail in this report, which provides an overview of how the excise tax is to be implemented. The information in the report is based on statute and guidance issued by the Department of the Treasury and the Internal Revenue Service.

The Patient Protection and Affordable Care Act (ACA; P.L. 111-148, as amended) includes a 40% excise tax on high-cost employer-sponsored health insurance coverage, often referred to as the *Cadillac tax*.[1] The 40% excise tax is assessed on the aggregate cost of employer-sponsored health coverage that exceeds a dollar limit. If a tax is owed, it is levied on the entity providing the coverage (e.g., the health insurance issuer or the employer). The excise tax goes into effect in 2018.

The excise tax is included in the ACA to raise revenue to offset the cost of other ACA provisions (e.g., the financial subsidies available through the health insurance exchanges), and it is expected to increase federal revenues by $87 billion between 2016 and 2025.[2] The excise tax also is expected to limit the tax advantages for employer-sponsored health coverage. Many economists contend that the tax advantages lead to an overconsumption of coverage and health care services.

This report provides an overview of the excise tax. The report includes cost estimates for the excise tax and explores the excise tax's relationship with the tax advantages for employer-sponsored health coverage. The information in this report is based on statute and two notices issued by the Department of the Treasury (Treasury) and the Internal Revenue Service (IRS). Notice 2015-16 was issued February 17, 2015, and the comment period for the notice closed May 15, 2015.[3] Notice 2015-52 was issued July 30, 2015. The comment period for the notice closes October 1, 2015.[4] As of the date of this report, regulations related to the excise tax have not been promulgated.

THE EXCISE TAX ON HIGH-COST EMPLOYER-SPONSORED HEALTH COVERAGE

Many employers offer health insurance plans and other health-related benefits (e.g., health care flexible spending accounts, or FSAs). These benefits are one part of an employee's total compensation. Often employers pay for part or all of these benefits. To illustrate, 55% of employers offered health insurance plans to their employees in 2014, and on average employers covered 82% of the premiums for single coverage and 71% of the premiums for family coverage.[5]

Beginning in 2018, a 40% excise tax is to be assessed on the aggregate cost of an employee's applicable coverage that exceeds a dollar limit during a taxable period.[6] Unlike some other ACA provisions, assessment of the excise tax is not dependent on an employer's characteristics (e.g., number of workers);[7]assessment is dependent on whether the aggregate cost of an employee's applicable coverage exceeds a dollar limit. The entity responsible for paying the excise tax to the IRS is the coverage provider. The terms *applicable coverage, dollar limit,* and *coverage provider* are defined and described in more detail below.

Definition of *Employee*

Under Section 4980I(d)(3) of the Internal Revenue Code (IRC), "the term employee includes any former employee, surviving spouse, or other primary insured individual." The same definition is used in this report unless otherwise noted.

Applicable Coverage

The excise tax is assessed on the amount by which the aggregate cost of an employee's *applicable coverage* exceeds a dollar limit.[8] The amount is called the *excess benefit.* Determining the excess benefit requires knowing which types of coverage are considered applicable coverage and how the cost of such coverage is calculated. For example, consider an employee who has an employer-sponsored health plan, a separate vision-only plan, and a health care flexible spending account (FSA). To determine the excess benefit, if any, of the employee's coverage, it is necessary to know whether any of the coverage is considered applicable coverage and the methods for determining the cost of such coverage.

Definition of Applicable Coverage

Applicable coverage is defined as

> coverage under any group health plan made available to the employee by an employer which is excludable from the employee's gross income under section 106 [of the IRC], or would be so excludable if it were employer-provided coverage (within the meaning of such section 106).[9]

Coverage that is excluded from an employee's gross income under Section 106 of the IRC includes, but is not limited to, employers' contributions to health insurance premiums, Archer Medical Savings Accounts (MSAs), and health savings accounts (HSAs).

Additionally, three arrangements are identified in the statute as applicable coverage:[10] (1) the employee-paid portion of health insurance coverage (i.e., an employee's contribution to premiums); (2) a self-employed individual's health insurance coverage for which a deduction is allowable under Section 162(l) of the IRC;[11] and (3) coverage under a group health plan for civilian employees of federal, state, or local governments. See *Table 1* for a list of what is considered applicable coverage based on the statute and Notice 2015-16.

Certain arrangements are excluded from the definition of applicable coverage (*Table 2*). Arrangements not considered applicable coverage are not included in the calculation for determining the aggregate cost of applicable coverage.

Determining the Cost of Applicable Coverage

The cost of applicable coverage is to be determined under rules "similar to" the rules in Section 4980B(f)(4) of the IRC.[12] These rules currently apply under Title X of the Consolidated Omnibus Budget Reconciliation Act of 1985 (COBRA; P.L. 99-272). Under COBRA, an employer with 20 or more employees that provided health insurance benefits must provide qualified employees and their families the option of continuing their coverage under the employer's group health insurance plan in certain cases where the employee's coverage otherwise would end (e.g., the employee is terminated). For COBRA purposes, the rules in Section 4980B(f)(4) of the IRC are used to determine the cost of the premium for the health insurance plan in which the former employee can continue.

Table 1. Applicable Coverage

(for purposes of the excise tax on high-cost employer-sponsored health coverage)

Employer's and employee's contributions to the premium for a group health plan
Retiree coverage
Health care flexible spending account (FSA)
Archer medical savings account (MSA)[a]
Health savings account (HSA)[b]
Health reimbursement account (HRA)[c]
On-site medical clinics[d]
Coverage for a specified disease or illness if the coverage or insurance is purchased with pretax dollars or able to be deducted under Section 162(l) of the IRC[e]
Hospital indemnity or other fixed indemnity insurance if the coverage or insurance is purchased with pretax dollars or able to be deducted under Section 162(l) of the IRC
Coverage for a self-employed individual, provided a deduction is allowable under Section 162(l) of the IRC
Coverage under a group health plan offered to civilians by a federal, state, or local government
Executive physical programs[f]

Sources: 26 U.S.C. §4980I; Notice 2015-16.

[a] In Notice 2015-16, Treasury and IRS indicate that they anticipate excluding employees' after-tax contributions to Archer MSAs from applicable coverage in future regulations.

[b] In Notice 2015-16, Treasury and IRS indicate that they anticipate excluding employees' after-tax contributions to HSAs from applicable coverage in future regulations.

[c] In Notice 2015-16, Treasury and IRS provide that they anticipate clarifying that HRAs are applicable coverage in future guidance.

[d] In Notice 2015-16, Treasury and IRS indicate that forthcoming proposed regulations will provide that on-site medical clinics that offer only de minimis medical care are not considered applicable coverage. Treasury and IRS requested comments on how to characterize the medical care provided by on-site medical clinics.

[e] IRC §162(l) allows self-employed individuals to deduct certain medical expenses, including premiums.

[f] In Notice 2015-16, Treasury and IRS provide that they anticipate clarifying that executive physical programs are applicable coverage in future guidance. A definition for an executive physical program is not provided.

Table 2. Not Considered Applicable Coverage
(for purposes of the excise tax on high-cost employer-sponsored health coverage)

Coverage only for accident or disability income insurance
Coverage issued as a supplement to liability insurance
Liability insurance (including general liability and automobile liability)
Workers' compensation or similar insurance
Automobile medical payment insurance
Credit-only insurance
Other coverage, as specified in regulations, that is secondary or incidental to other health insurance benefits
Coverage, whether through insurance or otherwise, for long-term care
Coverage under a separate policy for dental and/or vision care
Coverage for a specified disease or illness if the coverage or insurance is not excludable from gross income or a deduction under Section 162(l) of the IRC is not allowed with respect to it[a]
Hospital indemnity or other fixed indemnity insurance if the coverage or insurance is not excludable from gross income or a deduction under Section 162(l) of the IRC is not allowed with respect to it
Coverage under a plan offered to members of the military and their families by a federal, state, or local government
Employee after-tax contributions to HSAs and Archer MSAs[b]

Sources: 26 U.S.C. §4980I; Notice 2015-16.

[a] IRC §162(l) allows self-employed individuals to deduct certain medical expenses, including premiums.

[b] In Notice 2015-16, Treasury and IRS indicate that they anticipate excluding employees' after-tax contributions to HSAs and Archer MSAs from applicable coverage in future regulations.

As of the date of this report, information is not available about how the rules in Section 4980B(f)(4) of the IRC will be applied in the context of the excise tax. In Notice 2015-16, Treasury and IRS describe potential approaches they are considering for applying the COBRA rules to determine the cost of applicable coverage.[13]

The statute also includes specific calculation rules for determining the cost of applicable coverage:

- Any portion of the cost of applicable coverage that is attributable to the excise tax will not be taken into account.

- The cost of applicable coverage will be calculated separately for single coverage and non-single coverage (e.g., family coverage).[14]
- In the case of applicable coverage provided to retired employees, the plan can choose to treat a retired employee who is under the age of 65 and a retired employee aged 65 or older as similarly situated beneficiaries.[15]
- With respect to a health care FSA, the cost of applicable coverage is the greater of an employee's salary reduction election or the total reimbursements under the FSA.[16]
- With respect to Archer MSAs, the cost of applicable coverage is equal to an employer's contributions to the Archer MSA.[17]
- With respect to HSAs, the cost of applicable coverage is equal to an employer's contributions, including salary reduction contributions, to the HSA.[18]
- If the cost of applicable coverage is not determined on a monthly basis, the cost of the coverage will be allocated to months on a basis prescribed by the Secretary of the Treasury.

Dollar Limits

The excise tax is assessed on the excess benefit—the portion of an employee's applicable coverage that exceeds a dollar limit. In 2018, the dollar limits will be $10,200 for single coverage and $27,500 for non-single coverage (e.g., family coverage),[19] as adjusted by the health cost adjustment percentage. The health cost adjustment percentage is a one-time upward adjustment based on premium growth in the Blue Cross Blue Shield (BCBS) Standard plan under the Federal Employee Health Benefit (FEHB) program. The 2018 dollar limits will be adjusted upward if premium growth in the BCBS Standard plan is more than 55% between 2010 and 2018.[20]

In 2019, the limits will be the 2018 limits adjusted by the Consumer Price Index for all Urban Consumers (CPI-U) plus 1%.[21] In 2020 and beyond, the limits will be the previous year's limits adjusted by the CPI-U. The dollar limits also could be subject to two different adjustments, which are described below.

Demographic Adjustment

For some employers, the dollar limits for each year could be increased based on their employees' demographic characteristics. The adjustment could occur if the age and gender characteristics of all employees of an employer are significantly different from the age and gender characteristics of the national workforce.[22] The adjustment uses the BCBS Standard plan offered through the FEHB program. The cost of the BCBS Standard plan is determined based on the age and gender characteristics of the employer's workforce and on the age and gender characteristics of the national workforce. The amount the dollar limits could be increased is equal to the excess cost of the BCBS Standard plan adjusted for the employer's workforce as compared to the BCBS Standard plan adjusted for the national workforce.

Retiree and High-Risk Profession Adjustment

The limits also may be adjusted for (1) individuals who are qualified retirees and (2) individuals who participate in an employer-sponsored plan that has a majority of its enrollees engaged in a high-risk profession or "employed to repair or install electrical or telecommunications lines."[23] For purposes of this adjustment, *qualified retirees* are retired individuals aged 55 and older who do not qualify for Medicare. Employees engaged in *high-risk professions* are

> law enforcement officers (as such term is defined in section 1204 of the Omnibus Crime Control and Safe Streets Act of 1968), employees in fire protection activities (as such term is defined in section 3(y) of the Fair Labor Standards Act of 1938), individuals who provide out-of-hospital emergency medical care (including emergency medical technicians, paramedics, and first-responders), individuals whose primary work is longshore work (as defined in section 258(b) of the Immigration and Nationality Act (8 U.S.C. 1288(b)), determined without regard to paragraph (2) thereof), and individuals engaged in the construction, mining, agriculture (not including food processing), forestry, and fishing industries. Such term includes an employee who is retired from a high-risk profession described in the preceding sentence, if such employee satisfied the requirements of such sentence for a period of not less than 20 years during the employee's employment.[24]

Under this adjustment, the dollar limits are increased for these individuals by $1,650 for self-only coverage and $3,450 for coverage other than self-only.

Coverage Providers

The excise tax is not assessed on an employee; rather it is assessed on the entity providing the applicable coverage—the *coverage provider. Table 3* lists the coverage providers identified in statute.

Table 3. Coverage Provider by Type of Coverage
(for purposes of the excise tax on high-cost employer-sponsored health coverage)

Type of Coverage	Coverage Provider
Group health plan offered by a fully insured employer[a]	Health insurance issuer
Employer contributions to HSA	Employer
Employer contributions to Archer MSA	Employer
Other coverage (including coverage offered by a self- insured employer)[b]	Entity that administers the plan benefits[c]

Source: 26 U.S.C. §4980I(c)(2).

[a] A fully insured employer is one that purchased a health plan offered by a state-licensed insurance carrier.

[b] A self-insured employer sets aside funds to pay for health benefits directly and bears the risk for covering the medical expenses generated by the individuals covered under the self-insured plan.

[c] This term is not defined in statute, except to indicate that the term includes a plan sponsor if the plan sponsor administers the plan's benefits. In Notice 2015-52, Treasury and IRS explain the various approaches they are considering to identify the entity that administers the plan benefits.

It is possible that an employee's applicable coverage may not be provided by just one coverage provider. In the case of multiple coverage providers, each coverage provider is responsible for paying the excise tax on its *applicable share* of the excess benefit.[25] A coverage provider's applicable share is based on the cost of the coverage provider's applicable coverage in relation to the aggregate cost of all of the employee's applicable coverage.

In general, the employer is responsible for calculating the aggregate amount of applicable coverage that is in excess of the threshold and determining each coverage provider's applicable share of the tax.[26] The employer is required to notify the Secretary of the Treasury and each coverage provider about the amount determined. A penalty may be imposed on the employer if the excess benefit is not calculated correctly. The excise tax is nondeductible—coverage providers cannot deduct the excise tax as a business expense.

Cost Estimate

The excise tax is one of several taxes and fees included in the ACA to raise revenue to offset the cost of other ACA provisions (e.g., the financial subsidies available through the health insurance exchanges). In March 2015, the Congressional Budget Office (CBO) and the Joint Committee on Taxation (JCT) estimated the excise tax would increase federal revenues by $87 billion between 2016 and 2025.[27]

CBO and JCT indicate that the revenue raised by the excise tax will come from both collection of the excise tax and increases in taxable income, with most of the revenue raised a result of increases in taxable income.[28] The relationship between the excise tax and taxable income is discussed in the following section.

Relationship to the Tax Exclusion for Employer-Sponsored Insurance

Employer-sponsored health insurance and benefits generally are excluded from employees' gross income for purposes of determining employees' income tax liability.[29] Additionally, these amounts generally also qualify for exclusion from Social Security and Medicare (FICA) taxes and unemployment (FUTA) taxes.[30] These exclusions often are collectively referred to as the tax exclusion for employer-sponsored health insurance and benefits.

Modifying or repealing the tax exclusion has been discussed for many years. One reason federal policymakers are interested in the tax exclusion is that the exclusion results in considerable revenue loss to the federal government. JCT estimates the income tax exclusion will result in $785 billion in foregone revenue for the federal government between 2014 and 2018.[31] Ending or modifying the tax exclusion could raise a significant amount of revenue, depending on how it would be modified or repealed and how employers and workers would adjust.

The excise tax does not directly modify or end the tax exclusion; however, the excise tax is seen as an indirect method for limiting the tax exclusion. As discussed above, official scores indicate that the revenue raised by the excise tax will come both from collection of the excise tax and from increases in taxable income. The increases in taxable income are a result of the expectation that employers will reduce the amount of health coverage they offer to employees to avoid paying the excise tax. Provided employers do this but keep total compensation for employees constant (i.e., shift the compensation from health benefits to taxable wages), the result will be generally higher taxable wages for affected employees. CBO and JCT have estimated that about one-quarter of the revenue raised will come from collection of the excise tax, while about three-quarters of the revenue raised will stem from employers' responses to the tax.[32]

End Notes

[1] 26 U.S.C. §4890I.

[2] Congressional Budget Office, Insurance Coverage Provisions of the Affordable Care Act – CBO's March 2015 Baseline, March 9, 2015.

[3] Department of the Treasury (Treasury) and the Internal Revenue Service (IRS), Notice 2015-16, February 17, 2015.

[4] Treasury and IRS, Notice 2015-52, July 30, 2015.

[5] The Kaiser Family Foundation and Health Research & Educational Trust, Employer Health Benefits, 2014 Annual Survey, September 10, 2014.

[6] In statute, taxable period is defined as "the calendar year or such shorter period as the Secretary may prescribe. The Secretary may have different taxable periods for employers of varying sizes" (26 U.S.C. §4980I(f)(8)). In Notice 2015- 52, Treasury and IRS say that they anticipate the taxable period will be a calendar year for all taxpayers.

[7] For instance, the Patient Protection and Affordable Care Act (ACA; P.L. 111-148, as amended) employer shared responsibility requirement (the employer mandate) only applies to large employers as measured by the size of the employer's workforce.

[8] In Notice 2015-16, Treasury and IRS indicate that the aggregate cost of applicable coverage is based on the coverage in which the employee enrolls, not the coverage that is made available to the employee.

[9] 26 U.S.C. §4980I(d)(1)(A).

[10] 26 U.S.C. §4980I(d)(1).

[11] IRC §162(l) allows self-employed individuals to deduct certain medical expenses, including premiums.

[12] 26 U.S.C. §4980I(d)(2).

[13] See the "Determination of Cost of Applicable Coverage" section of Notice 2015-16.

[14] See 26 U.S.C. §4980I(f)(1)(B) for the definition of non-single coverage.

[15] Under Consolidated Omnibus Budget Reconciliation Act of 1985 (COBRA; P.L. 99-272) rules, a former employee's premium is based on the cost of coverage for "similarly situated" non-COBRA beneficiaries. These similarly situated individuals are employees and their dependents who are receiving coverage from the employer and were most similarly

situated to the COBRA beneficiary prior to the COBRA beneficiary becoming a former employee.

[16] Total reimbursements under a flexible spending account (FSA) may be greater than an employee's salary reduction election if an employer makes nonelective contributions (often referred to as flex credits) to the employee's FSA and the employee uses those funds.

[17] In Notice 2015-16, Treasury and IRS indicate that they anticipate excluding employees' after-tax contributions to Archer medical savings accounts (MSAs) from applicable coverage in future regulations.

[18] In Notice 2015-16, Treasury and IRS indicate that they anticipate excluding employees' after-tax contributions to health savings accounts (HSAs) from applicable coverage in future regulations.

[19] Any coverage provided under a multiemployer plan (as defined in IRC §414(f)) is treated as coverage other than single coverage. In other words, coverage provided under a multiemployer plan is always subject to the non-single coverage threshold.

[20] Currently, it seems unlikely that premium growth in the Blue Cross Blue Shield Standard plan will exceed 55% between 2010 and 2018, as premium growth between 2010 and 2015 was about 20% for both the single and family coverage options. Premium growth for 2016 through 2018 would have to be significantly higher than in recent years for growth over the whole period to exceed 55%.

[21] The Consumer Price Index for All Urban Consumers (CPI-U) is a measure of inflation published by the U.S. Bureau of Labor Statistics.

[22] The term national workforce is not defined in statute. Treasury and IRS explain an approach they are considering to determine the characteristics of the national workforce in Notice 2015-52.

[23] 26 U.S.C. §4980I(b)(3)(C)(iv).

[24] 26 U.S.C. §4980I(f)(3).

[25] 26 U.S.C. §4980I(c).

[26] For multiemployer plans, the plan sponsor has this responsibility.

[27] Congressional Budget Office, Insurance Coverage Provisions of the Affordable Care Act - CBO's March 2015 Baseline, March 9, 2015.

[28] Congressional Budget Office, Updated Estimates of the Effects of the Insurance Coverage Provisions of the Affordable Care Act, April 2014, April 14, 2014, at http://www.cbo.gov/publication/45231.

[29] 26 U.S.C. §§105(b) and 106.

[30] 26 U.S.C. §§3121(a)(2), 3306(b)(2).

[31] Joint Committee on Taxation, Estimates of Federal Tax Expenditures for Fiscal Years 2014-2018, August 5, 2014. This estimate does not include the effect of the exclusion for employment taxes.

[32] Congressional Budget Office, Updated Estimates of the Effects of the Insurance Coverage Provisions of the Affordable Care Act, April 2014, April 14, 2014, at http://www.cbo.gov/publication/45231.

INDEX

E

F

G

H

V

W